A Mind Of Her Own

A Mind
Of Her Own

A Life of
the Writer George Sand

---

by Tamara Hovey

Illustrated with photographs

HARPER & ROW, PUBLISHERS
New York, Hagerstown, San Francisco, London

Frontispiece: George Sand at thirty-three.
Painting by Auguste Charpentier.

Carnavalet Museum, *photo Archives Photographiques—Paris*

A Mind of Her Own: A Life of the Writer George Sand
Copyright © 1977 by Tamara Hovey

FIRST EDITION

Library of Congress Cataloging in Publication Data
Hovey, Tamara.
    A mind of her own.

    SUMMARY: A biography of the nineteenth-century
French author who defied many social conventions in
order to live and write as she wanted.
    1. Sand, George, pseud. of Mme. Dudevant, 1804–1876—
Juvenile literature.   2. Novelists, French—19th century
—Biography—Juvenile literature.   [1. Sand, George,
pseud. of Mme. Dudevant, 1804–1876]   I. Title.
PQ2412.H58   843'.8   [B]   [92]   76–24310
ISBN 0–06–022616–1
ISBN 0–06–022617–X lib. ed.

To the memory of Sonya Levien

Contents

Author's Note
ix

George Sand's World
1

A Mind of Her Own
4

Bibliography
204

Index
207

Author's Note

On the edge of the village of Nohant in France, George Sand's home still stands. In its furnishings and in the disposition of its spacious grounds, its original character has been preserved for a century. A few miles away, the town of La Châtre harbors a George Sand Museum containing family portraits and papers, while in the monastery at Valldemosa on the island of Majorca, stone walls are covered with reminders of her passage there. The principal libraries of Paris possess first editions of her works, her manuscripts and unpublished diaries, as well as the letters of nineteenth-century figures who were her friends. All these repositories offer rich veins of source material upon which I have drawn in the preparation of this book. The dialogue and quotations which appear in the text come from original sources; only the translations are my own.

For the better part of four decades, Georges Lubin

has devoted himself to the discovery and compilation of George Sand's extraordinarily voluminous correspondence, enriching the collection with his notes and valuable comments. The profundity and extent of M. Lubin's knowledge, the flawless integrity he has brought to his annotated two-volume edition of George Sand's autobiographical writings, have made of it in a sense a biography, unrivaled for its authenticity, of a major portion of her life. To his inspired scholarship I owe an immeasurable debt.

I am grateful as well to M. Marcel Thomas, Keeper of Manuscripts at the Bibliothèque Nationale in Paris, and to M. Jacques Suffel of the Bibliothèque Spoelberch de Lovenjoul in Chantilly, for allowing me to consult the manuscripts and documents kept in their charge. For showing me through the vault in which reside original editions, family photographs and memorabilia turned over to the city of Paris by George Sand's granddaughter Aurore Lauth-Sand, I wish to thank Mlle. Marie-Thérèse Liégeas of the Bibliothèque Historique de la Ville de Paris. I am grateful to Señora Margarita Ferrá for giving me the opportunity of studying the manuscripts and drawings belonging to the Frédéric Chopin-George Sand cell at the Charterhouse of Valldemosa. For his unfailing patience in responding to my questions, I wish to thank M. Robert Franco, the conscientious and devoted keeper of George Sand's home at Nohant.

I owe special thanks to M. Jacques Wilhelm, Chief Curator of the Carnavalet Museum in Paris, for his kindness in guiding me to nineteenth-century paintings and drawings. I am indebted for research assistance to

Mme. Geneviève Gareau of the Service Photographique at the Caisse Nationale des Monuments Historiques. I wish to thank Howard Greenfeld for his advice and encouragement, and I am deeply grateful to Elaine Edelman for her creative editorial help.

George Sand's World

George Sand came into the world in 1832, not as mortals usually come into it—as tiny, helpless, speechless objects—but as a fully formed and articulate adult of twenty-eight, wearing trousers, tie and a top hat. Possessing no ancestors, the offspring of no parents—and not even a man, despite her name—George Sand was the unique personality which a gifted Frenchwoman called Aurore Dupin invented for herself when she published her first novel.

She chose to disguise herself with the name and clothes of a man for a compelling reason. Like other women of her day, Aurore Dupin had been born in a prison. The bars were invisible, made not of iron but of prejudice, while the gates were heavily guarded by age-long tradition. For the poorer inmates of this social prison, existence was often a life sentence of drudgery in peasant huts and in the fields of wealthy landowners who could use them as brutally as they wished. But the more well-to-do were often no less condemned . . . to loveless, arranged marriages, to empty hours of quasi-idleness bent over embroideries destined to decorate houses of which they, the mistresses, were hardly more than decorations themselves. There seemed no escape to a different and richer life.

And yet with the most innocent of devices—pen and paper and the pseudonym of a man—Aurore Dupin walked past the unsuspecting guardians of tradition and out through the barred gates forever. The story of her life is the story of her imprisonment, of her escape, and of the world she discovered "on the outside" and made her own.

This world was the France of men of genius—of Honoré de Balzac, Gustave Flaubert, Alexandre Dumas the younger, Frédéric Chopin, Franz Liszt, Alfred de Musset—some of whom were George Sand's lovers, all of whom were her intimate friends. She was considered their peer and she became one of the most widely read and influential writers of her day, an outstanding representative of the Romantic Movement in literature.

Hers was the France, as well, of powerful empires . . . of shattering military defeats . . . of political ferment and repression . . . of revolutions. In the forefront of the struggles for freedom in her day, George Sand played a unique role. And in the area of women's rights she championed ideas which were far ahead of her time.

Hers was the France, too, of the hills and farms of the province of Berry, where she grew up and spent most of her adult life. It was a country from which she drew inspiration for the formidable body of writing—over one hundred volumes of novels, plays and memoirs—which led her contemporaries to call her "the great woman of the century."

It was a France, above all, from which George Sand emerged as something more than French, something more than a writer. Her achievements are proof that the mind has no gender, and she herself has become a symbol of the independent spirit that lies hidden perhaps in every man—and every woman.

1

In a shabby Paris apartment on a day early in the nineteenth century, a small girl was standing on a cold foot warmer inside a playpen her mother had devised out of four old cane-bottomed chairs. She was making up a story and she had been reciting it for hours. Her aunt, who was visiting with the little girl's mother, eyed the child impatiently.

"Aurore," she demanded, "how long is that princess of yours going to take to put on her golden crown?"

"Oh, let her alone," Aurore's mother said. "The only time I can work in peace is when she is safely inside those four chairs making up one of her novels."

The "novel" was actually a fairy tale inspired by pictures in a book the girl's mother had read to her. And as Aurore Dupin, who would grow up to be known as George Sand, recollected years later, there was a good deal of truth to her mother's words. Inventing tales had

4

absorbed her completely and kept her out of mischief. The princes and princesses who peopled them were as real to her as her own family. The marble palaces in which they lived seemed as familiar to her as her own one-room apartment with the small bed tucked away in a corner by day and drawn out at night for her to sleep in, or the iron stove where a pot was usually simmering with sugared milk soup for her dinner.

Aurore spent most of the first four years of her life in this Paris apartment on the rue de la Grange-Batelière. Beyond its curtained window lay the slate gray rooftops and chimney pots of the capital of France, where she had been born on July 1, 1804. Somewhere out there lived the fashionable ladies for whom Aurore's mother, Sophie Dupin, had sewn gowns of silk and satin in a shop she kept before her marriage. A pretty woman with a slender, graceful figure, Sophie had rarely been able to afford anything finer for herself, however, than dresses of plain percale.

Money was always a problem in the Dupin family, and yet Aurore's father, Maurice Dupin, came of a well-to-do background. A handsome young man, with dark velvety eyes which his daughter inherited, he was an officer in the French army who had distinguished himself on the battlefield. In this respect, he took after his famous grandfather, for whom he had been named— Maurice, the Count de Saxe, Marshal of France under King Louis XV. The Count de Saxe had become renowned for his heroism during the War of the Austrian Succession in the eighteenth century, a period of rivalry among monarchies.

Wars were a frequent occurrence then; so were illegitimate children of royal blood. Aurore's grand-mother on her father's side, for instance, was the illegitimate daughter of the Count de Saxe, who was an illegitimate son of the King of Poland as well as an illegitimate great uncle of three kings of France. And none of this was really considered a disgrace. A disgrace there had been, however, and it was a terrible one in the eyes of the French aristocracy. It had fallen upon the family when Maurice Dupin contracted a *legitimate* marriage with Aurore's mother, for he was a nobleman and she was a commoner—her father had been a bird keeper who sold canaries on a Paris quay.

When Maurice's widowed mother learned of the marriage, which had been performed without her knowledge, she refused to have anything to do with her son's lowborn wife. Living far away from Paris on her beautiful country estate, she confined herself to sending her son a meager allowance which scarcely paid for his military wardrobe.

Sophie pretended not to care that she was rejected by her husband's proud parent. She was proud too . . . deeply proud of her own origins. As George Sand would later write of her mother: "She belonged to the People to the tips of her fingers and in this she felt herself to be more noble than all the patricians and the aristocrats of the earth."

Since Aurore's father was often away with the army, the child spent her days for the most part with her mother. Sophie Dupin, with her lively dark eyes, with her black ringlets billowing out from beneath the frilled edges of her bonnet, was a youthful mother despite her thirty-odd years. Sometimes she would take her little

Aurore's mother, Sophie Dupin. Pencil sketch drawn by George Sand in 1833.

Aurore's father, Maurice Dupin.

daughter for walks in the countryside. A thoroughgoing city woman, she was always naively struck with the sights around them and never failed to share her delight over "a beautiful cloud, a striking sun effect, the clear water of a running stream"—as George Sand later recalled. "And suddenly those objects, which I might never have noticed by myself, were revealed to me in all their beauty. It was as if my mother possessed a magic key which opened up my mind."

Before Maurice Dupin and Sophie met, Maurice had fathered an illegitimate son whom his aristocratic mother was raising in the countryside. Sophie also had an illegitimate child, Caroline. Sometimes Aurore's half sister, who was five years older, would come home from the school where she boarded. Then the couch would be turned into a temporary bed for Caroline and placed alongside Aurore's little cot. But more often than not Aurore would simply sit at home alone within her four cane-bottomed chairs, weaving tales about her beautiful princesses and make-believe palaces.

When she was almost four years old, she went to live for a while in a real palace. Her father was stationed in Spain and her mother, pregnant again, decided to journey there with Aurore to join him. Maurice Dupin was serving as aide-de-camp to the Commander-in-Chief of the French forces in Spain, Joachim Murat. Murat and his staff were quartered in a royal palace in Madrid, and so Sophie and Aurore stayed there as well.

Aurore was too young to question why the French army was occupying a foreign country. All of Europe knew, however, for it had been witnessing the growing power of the Emperor of France, Napoleon Bonaparte, for nearly fifteen years. Napoleon had moved his armies ruthlessly across Europe, taking over one country after another. Early in 1808 he removed the royal family from the throne of Spain and placed Murat in charge of the Spanish government. It was now spring of 1808 and Napoleon held almost the entire continent under his domination and was threatening England with invasion.

The Emperor was confident of the future, for he had the bourgeoisie—the rich industrial class—of France behind him. As George Sand later wrote, however, "he mistook the aspirations of a class for the aspirations of humanity." He did not suspect that most Spaniards hated him as much as they loved their own liberty. He seemed to have no notion that, beyond the walls of the beautiful palace where Aurore and her parents were living, the Spanish people were secretly collecting arms with which to drive his French soldiers from their country.

During her two months in Madrid, Aurore wandered at will through the spacious rooms which had only recently been occupied by the Queen of Spain. Her mother often left her to play alone, for Sophie was confined to her bed after giving birth to Aurore's brother Louis. His birth made little impression on Aurore, nor did the fact that he was born blind, for this was a tragedy she could not comprehend. But she was entranced with her surroundings where "everything was gilded and appeared to me to be made of solid gold, as it always is in fairy tales."

There was something awe-inspiring in the silence in the pillared halls of the palace. Oil portraits of royal personages seemed to come out from their frames and to follow Aurore with their eyes. She escaped from them to the vast terrace which fronted the square, to discover that there too all was still. She was too tiny to look over the balustrade, so she peered between its white marble columns. One day she spied the familiar figure of her father's manservant, Weber, crossing the square below, and she called out his name. He did not hear her, but a few instants later "Weber!" came back to her from the other end of the empty balcony in a voice which seemed a double of her own. Her mother, who was always careful not to check the flight of the child's imagination, told her that it was a voice called Echo which lived in the air.

Aurore's explorations of her new home were brought abruptly to an end one day when the serenity of the royal apartments was disturbed by the sound of cannons. There was great confusion in the palace. French soldiers seized their guns as word spread that the Spanish people had risen in rebellion against the French. Bags were hastily packed and Aurore was bundled with her mother and infant brother into a coach her father had procured. Soon they were fleeing "along the road to France across a Spain in flames."

Murat's army retreated before the pursuing Spaniards, and the coach with Aurore and Sophie and the baby in it followed in the wake of the fighting forces. When the horses needed to rest, Sophie and the children would stop at some half-demolished inn to spend the night. Once Aurore found herself sitting at a window, watching what seemed the most fabulous display of fireworks she had ever seen.

"It's a battle," came her mother's voice at her side,

"and your father, perhaps, is fighting in it."

Aurore went on watching and peacefully eating an apple.

"How lucky children are to understand nothing," Sophie sighed as she lifted the little girl in her arms and laid her down to sleep on a makeshift bed.

Sophie and Aurore and the baby rode on over abandoned battlefields through an epidemic-ridden countryside. All three contracted a skin disease which caused them to break out in red blotches. The baby became feverish. Aurore burned with a thirst that nothing could quench. They picked their way among dead bodies strewn over the fields, but they could not drink the water in the rain-filled ditches for the clots of blood floating in it.

Worst of all for Aurore was the hunger which never left her night or day and which an occasional lemon or onion or handful of sunflower seeds did little to assuage. Once some French soldiers by the edge of the road offered her a portion of a thick liquid they were drinking. There were little bits of blackened string in it, for it had been made from boiled candle ends. Aurore gulped it down ravenously.

As they approached the French border, the fighting diminished and Aurore's father, granted a leave, was able to join his wife and children. The reunited family traveled in the same battered coach toward the sea. They ate and slept in clean inns now, and washed the vermin from their clothes. When they reached the coast, Aurore's father hired a boat to carry them and their coach across the Bay of Biscay to France. The children were still feverish and covered with a rash, but they were being carefully treated by Sophie with ill-smelling sulphur powder. It seemed that the perils of the journey were over.

As the boat entered the mouth of the Gironde river in France, however, it struck a reef. Water flooded the deck and the boat began to capsize. Aurore became aware of the panic about her as the pilot and his assistant lost control. Then she became aware of something else . . . of the sure, lithe figure of her father, the gold fringe on the scarlet sash of his uniform gleaming in the sunlight. He seized the wheel and guided the sinking hulk toward shore.

When the coach took to the road again, Maurice Dupin turned the horses toward central France and his mother's country estate in Nohant. A little village in the province of Berry, Nohant lay in the heart of *la Vallée Noire*—the Black Valley. The trees blanketing the valley were of so deep a green that from a distance they appeared almost black. On the edge of the village of Nohant were the large comfortable house and rambling gardens which belonged to Aurore's grandmother. They were surrounded by fields cultivated by peasants whose labor brought in the revenues that supported the estate.

Before leaving Madrid, Maurice had written his mother; and now the elder Madame Dupin—Madame Dupin de Francueil, as she was always called—was waiting impatiently. The lonely widow had at last realized that the love and companionship of her only son were more important to her than her aristocratic prejudices. She had made up her mind to welcome his wife and children.

Aurore spent the journey tossing in a feverish sleep and awoke just as the dusty coach arrived in the courtyard at Nohant. She felt overawed by her grandmother's imposing air. "She was dressed, as she invariably was, in a long-waisted brown silk dress with flat sleeves. Her blond wig which frizzed up into a little billow over her forehead, and her tiny round bonnet which mounted into a lace peak, made of her a singular being who resembled no one I had ever seen before."

Madame Dupin de Francueil embraced Maurice, called Sophie "daughter," and urged the two young parents to take the baby with them to their quarters to rest. Then she glanced down at the dark-eyed girl who looked so like her son.

"I'll take charge of this one," she said.

She did not seem to notice the red blotches or the muddy shoes or the rotten-egg smell of sulphur about Aurore, but picked her up tenderly. She carried her to a room which "seemed to me like something out of paradise. The walls were covered with Persian cloth with a large floral pattern. All the furniture dated from the time of Louis XV. The bed, which was shaped like a hearse with great plumes at its four corners, was hung with double curtains and covered with a quantity of pillows and embroidered fittings whose exquisite luxury filled me with wonder. I did not dare lie down on such a beautiful thing for I realized the disgust which my appearance must inspire. But my grandmother made me quickly forget this by her kindness and affection."

When Aurore awoke a few hours later, the first person she saw was a sturdy nine-year-old boy, her half

The family house at Nohant.

brother. He came into the room with an enormous bouquet of flowers, which he tossed at her.

"This is Hippolyte," her grandmother announced.
"Kiss each other, my children. . . ."

As the children embraced dutifully, Aurore heard her
mother say to her father, "Well, he shall be mine, too,
just as Caroline is yours." Thus Sophie bound her husband's illegitimate son and her own illegitimate daughter into a family of four children she hoped would live
happily together.

But Grandmother Dupin de Francueil refused to extend her liberality to include Caroline. And little Louis,
wasted with fever and exhaustion, died within a few
days. He was buried beneath the tall cypresses in the
family cemetery. Her parents hid their grief from
Aurore, who seemed so enchanted with her grandmother's home.

Aurore wandered through the bright rooms on the
ground floor or climbed the high, curving staircase to
the top. There she came upon windows which framed
the courtyard and, beyond, the little village church with
its tiled belfry. When the cook's back was turned, she
and Hippolyte baked mud pies in the great iron stove
in the kitchen, where the walls were hung with gleaming
copper pots. With her brother as guide, she explored
the vast grounds outside. They were beautiful and untamed, with winding paths bordered with banks of vio-
lets and primroses which pushed their way lushly up to
the very edge of the woods. Occasionally the little girl
would pause to gaze curiously at an eccentric old man
who wore white stockings and gaiters. His name was
Deschartres, and years before he had been her father's

15

tutor. Now the crotchety but kindhearted Deschartres managed the estate at Nohant and was considered almost a member of the family.

Hardly a week after the baby's death, another tragedy overtook Nohant. One night, Maurice Dupin was galloping back from the neighboring town of La Châtre, where he had gone to dine with boyhood friends. He was riding a horse named Leopardo, which he had received as a gift from the deposed King of Spain. Leopardo was a wild and high-strung animal, and when he came upon a heap of stones lying beyond a sharp curve in the road, he shied. Aurore's father was thrown to the ground and instantly killed.

Madame Dupin de Francueil, whom even a short walk in the garden left drained of her strength, walked over two miles that night in a driving rainstorm in her bedroom slippers to the roadside where Maurice lay. As a carriage bore her back to Nohant, "the poor mother prostrated herself on the body of her son and groaned as if in a death agony of her own." Sophie's grief was no less violent.

Aurore was terrified when her mother tried to make her put on black stockings and she tearfully refused to wear "the legs of a dead person." Only when Sophie showed her that everyone in the house wore black did the child give in. Still she could not understand the meaning of her father's death and kept asking her mother, "Is my father still dead today?"

At Nohant during the next few years "the only laughter that was heard in that house of mourning was the laughter of children." Aurore played with Hippolyte,

16

racing him down the garden or climbing trees with him like a tomboy. She found a new pastime which delighted her: she learned to write and to read by copying printed letters from books. But at the age of seven she was still a child who loved to daydream. She would leave her boisterous games with her brother to sit for hours on a stool at her mother's or her grandmother's feet, lost in a trance, her mouth half open, an almost stupid expression on her face. "I have always seen her like that," her mother was quick to explain to her grandmother. "It's not stupidity, it's her nature. She doesn't speak but, as her poor father used to say, don't imagine she is not thinking about something for all that."

Aurore's grandmother, "serious and calm, had the dignified manners of the nobility and a quiet protective goodness about her." Aurore's mother was "hot-blooded by nature, ever ready to break out into a storm." Despite the difference in their characters, the elder and younger Dupin women were drawn together by their shared grief. Gradually, however, a rivalry began to develop between them over Aurore. "They needed to love me and to spoil me to console themselves for their painful loss."

Aurore's grandmother wanted the child to develop a logical and scientific bent of mind. She was a disciple of Voltaire and of Jean-Jacques Rousseau, philosophers of the eighteenth-century Enlightenment who had rejected religious dogma and championed human reason. Aurore's mother, on the other hand, had an emotional faith in the supernatural, "like the peasant who bows

17

Aurore's grandmother, Madame Dupin de Francueil.

down now before God, now before the devil, sometimes mistaking one for the other." She wanted Aurore
to share her own mystical feelings. Aurore's grandmother believed in "an acquired grace—in learning
how to walk in a special way, how to sit, how to hold a
fork." She wanted to inculcate these manners in
Aurore. Her mother, who had a natural grace of her
own, "found all that sort of thing mightily ridiculous."
She wanted the girl raised to simple country ways. The
grandmother wanted . . . The mother wanted . . . And
Aurore began to feel as if the two women "were fighting
a desperate battle over the bits and pieces of my heart."

She had no difficulty in making a choice between
them. Her mother had a quick temper and a quick hand
when she scolded, but she as quickly made up afterward
with comforting caresses. Her grandmother never laid
a finger on her; when she disapproved of something
Aurore did, she confined herself to a cool word of repri-
mand. Her grandmother seemed an awesome stranger
by comparison to the mother she adored.

One day she overheard her grandmother persuading
Sophie to sign over Aurore's legal guardianship in exchange for an allowance which she would provide for
Sophie in Paris. Aurore clung to her mother, "covering
her with kisses and begging her not to give me away to
my grandmother for money." Sophie tried to explain
that her grandmother had promised to bring Aurore up
to Paris for visits, and in the summers she herself would
come back to Nohant. But the girl sobbed wretchedly
when she saw Sophie packing her bags, and she begged
her mother to take her along with her.

"If I took you with me, your grandmother would

reduce my allowance. We would be so poor you would not be able to bear it and you would ask for your No-hant again."

"Never! Never!" answered Aurore in anguish. "We'll be poor, but we'll be together. We'll work, we'll eat beans and live in an attic—what's wrong with that? We'll be happy and no one will be able to stop us from loving each other!"

But the next morning, before Aurore was up, Sophie slipped away from Nohant. She hated to leave her little daughter, but there was her older daughter to think of, too. Aurore's grandmother flatly refused to have Caroline at Nohant, yet Sophie could not leave her in boarding school indefinitely. As Sophie's carriage sped away, she could console herself with the thought that at least Aurore would not be raised in poverty, as she herself had been.

Her mother's absence from Nohant plunged Aurore into fits of melancholy, but she still found much to fascinate her in the life on her grandmother's estate. She did not enjoy the strict lessons in good manners she received from her grandmother. She did not take much pleasure, either, in the hours she spent, along with Hippolyte, learning Latin, history and natural science from the exacting old tutor Deschartres, "who had a gift for making the most interesting subjects boring." But even Deschartres could not spoil her love for books and, thanks to her grandmother, she discovered a new love.

Madame Dupin de Francueil was an accomplished musician. Though her fingers were stiffening with age and her voice was failing, she could sing with the truest

Aurore as a child. Pastel by her grandmother.

and purest of tones. While the old lady accompanied herself on the harpsichord, Aurore would sit on the floor beneath the instrument, sharing a corner of the rug with her grandmother's dog, Brillant. Her grandmother would sing arias from the old Italian masters and Aurore would listen "in absolute ecstacy. I could have passed every day of my life there, so caught was I in the spell of that quavering voice and the strident twang of the old harpsichord." Her grandmother began to teach Aurore the fundamentals of music and to sing little duets with her. Before long the girl's grandmother had taught her how to play the harpsichord and the harp as well.

When Aurore was eleven, her brother, Hippolyte, was sent off to join the cavalry, so she lost a companion. But she had many others in the peasant children who lived around Nohant. Tagging along with them to their thatch-roofed houses, she learned how to milk a cow, help gather in the harvest, capture wild birds. On moonlight nights the peasant women would collect in the village square. While they pounded the flax which would later make their homespun garments, they told stories in relays. Aurore sat listening with fascination to the tales of monsters and demons that were part of their folklore. She hid this fascination from her grandmother, however. She knew the rational old lady strongly disapproved of superstition.

As she approached her teens, Aurore began to change rapidly. She had not given up thinking out long "novels" in her head, but now she tried to set her thoughts down on paper as well. She wrote about the way the Black Valley appeared from the hills where she used to take her walks, and her indulgent grandmother found her descriptions little "masterpieces." She grew robust and healthy, adding to her height until she reached, at thirteen, the five foot two she would remain the rest of her life. The tawny skin she had inherited from her mother had a new bloom, and her large dark eyes bore the fresh luster of girlhood.

The world around her was changing as well. Napoleon's glory had begun to diminish dramatically. The Emperor had wanted to conquer Russia in order to use its strength to help him invade England. Now starving remnants of his army, which had been decimated on the Russian front, had straggled back to France to wander in rags over the countryside. His dreams of conquest had been shattered along with his armies. In 1815 the British defeated Napoleon decisively at Waterloo in Belgium and deported him to the island of Saint Helena, where he remained until his death. The Emperor's collapse was followed by the Restoration in France, a period which was to last fifteen years. It "restored" elements in the country which the idealistic French revolutionaries of 1789 had thought they had banished forever: the monarchy, the aristocracy and the influence of the clergy.

Grandmother Dupin, bending her freethinking, Voltairean ways to the new conservative times, decided that for the sake of appearances Aurore should take her First Communion. The girl went through the ceremony with the gentle though superficial obedience which had become a habit with her by now. She was puzzled by the behavior of her grandmother, whom she had never seen set foot in a church before. But she did not express her puzzlement. It had become a habit with her, too, to keep her feelings to herself, for she was aware of the differences they might stir up between her mother and her grandmother when the two women met in Paris, or during Sophie's occasional visits to Nohant.

The jealous antagonism between her mother and grandmother, though veiled by outward politeness and even grudging mutual respect, had continued over the years. It caused Aurore to feel a need for "a go-between, an intermediary, someone half man, half god . . . who would be uncritical, indulgent, good." Unable to discover such a creature in real life, she fashioned one out of her imagination. She called him Corambé, and she built a temple of stones and moss to him in a hidden corner of the garden. She wove long novels in her head about this kindly, understanding, all-forgiving being until it often seemed to her as if he were more tangible than the flesh-and-blood people around her.

But for all that Corambé became a solace to her, he was no substitute for her mother. Aurore longed to abandon her future as heiress of Nohant in order to live with Sophie in Paris. She did not speak of this to her grandmother, for she knew how much it would wound her. The aging woman had never recovered from the death of her only child, and at odd moments she called Aurore "Maurice" or said to her abstractedly, "Come here, my son. . . ."

One day when Aurore emerged from her grandmother's room, where she had been scolded for being inattentive in her studies, she was so upset she flung her books to the floor. She thought she was alone, and she covered her face with her hands, groaning, "I don't study because I don't want to. I have my reasons. I'll tell them some day."

Her grandmother's maid, Julie, suddenly appeared behind her.

"You are a bad child," she reprimanded Aurore. "You could be forgiven for acting lazy, but to do so on purpose . . . ? You deserve to be sent back to your mother!"

"My mother?" returned Aurore. "Sent back to my mother? But that's all I want, that's all I ask!"

Julie bore Aurore's words to Madame Dupin de Francueil, who gave orders that the girl be kept in her room for three days. She was permitted to leave it only to take her meals alone or to go for a brief walk in the garden.

Distraught, Aurore escaped from the house whenever she could. On one of her walks, she encountered an old peasant woman struggling to pick up a bundle of wood which was too heavy for her. Aurore slung the wood over her own shoulders and carried it to the woman's hut. Then she sat on a stone outside the door eating a slice of dark bread the peasant woman had given her. The first stars were twinkling in the sky, the blackbirds were singing in the neighboring woods, and Aurore wished this moment of freedom might last forever. "No more dreary lessons," she thought. "No more sickly-sweet jams which you have to pretend to like so you won't seem ungrateful. No more strict hours for dining or sleeping or playing. No lackey to hand you your plate or to whisk it away before you have finished. No one to tell you to put on your shawl or you'll catch cold. No one to . . ." But her reverie was cut short when a maid from Nohant came to fetch her and she was shut back up in her room.

Aurore was grieved to have hurt her grandmother, and when she was sent for at last, she hurried to the old lady's side. She was utterly unprepared for the scene that followed.

> I was on my knees by her bed and I had taken her hands in mine to kiss them, when she spoke in a voice which throbbed with a bitterness which made it unrecognizable.
>
> "Stay on your knees and listen to me carefully, for what I am going to say you have never heard from my lips before and never will again. . . ."
>
> After this preamble, which sent a shudder through me, she began to recount the story of my mother's life, the story, at least, as she understood it, as she interpreted it.

Madame Dupin de Francueil told her a sorry tale of the sort of woman she felt Sophie Dupin was . . . with her illegitimate child, Caroline, with other illegitimate relationships, past and present, which were hinted at darkly. Only years later did Aurore, now George Sand, understand enough to write about it.

> She told it without pity and without wisdom. For, if I may say so, in the life of the poor there are temptations, misfortunes, fatalities which the rich can never understand and which they judge no better than a blind man is able to judge colors. . . . Speaking in a choked voice, she unleashed the awful, the frightful words; my mother was a lost woman and I a blind child who was throwing myself into an abyss.
>
> It was like a nightmare to me. My throat tightened. Each word made something in me die. I broke into a sweat. I wanted to interrupt, I wanted to rise, to go away,

to reject with horror these frightful confidences. I couldn't. I was glued there on my knees, racked and bent by this voice which floated over me, drying me up like a summer wind. . . .

Finally I rose without a word, without seeking a caress or asking forgiveness. I went back up to my room . . . and rolled on the floor in sobbing convulsions.

For weeks afterward, Aurore went about with red-rimmed but dry eyes, too proud to reveal her unhappiness. Only to her imaginary god Corambé did she confide her thoughts. Strangely enough, she found that she still loved both her mother and her grandmother. Yet if her mother was as contemptible as her grandmother had said, it seemed to her that she, her mother's daughter, must be contemptible too. What was the use of doing anything to improve herself? She found more hateful than ever the idea of becoming "a beautiful young miss, dainty, affected and erudite, who played the piano for people who nodded approvingly without listening or understanding—a girl who cared for no one but herself and for nothing but the admiration of others and whose sole aim was a rich marriage in which she would sell her liberty and her individuality for a carriage, a coat of arms and a few bits of lace."

Fleeing the house whenever she could, she lived in the fields, playing noisy games with the peasant children. Even when she played by herself at home she was rowdy and ungovernable. She stubbornly refused to put her mind to her studies. And she became a wild, rebellious creature beholden, she felt, to no one.

Her grandmother at last took stern measures. She informed Aurore that she would soon be leaving with her for Paris to place her in school in a convent.

"Will I be allowed to see my mother?"

"Yes, certainly, you will see her," her grandmother answered coldly, "after which you will be separated from her—and from me—for whatever time is required for you to finish your education."

Aurore had one last hope—that her mother would stand up to her grandmother. But Sophie Dupin was in no position to oppose Madame Dupin de Francueil. When Aurore arrived in Paris, she was lectured by her mother on the advantages of being wealthy and educated. The girl felt totally rejected.

The next day was a wintry day. "I was made to dress in a purple serge uniform, my things were placed in a valise, and I was driven in a horse-drawn carriage to the rue des Fossés-Saint-Victor," George Sand recalled later. "After waiting a few minutes in an anteroom, someone opened a communicating door, which closed behind me. I was cloistered."

2

Aurore entered the Convent of the Dames Augustines Anglaises in 1818. It was a retreat for English women who had taken the veil, as well as an exclusive school for young girls from across the English Channel and for the daughters of the French nobility.

Nestled among old buildings on the Left Bank of the Seine, the convent was like a city within a city—a stone-walled enclave of vaulted cloisters and dingy classrooms, of bare cells and frigid dormitories, of spacious gardens planted with chestnut trees and kitchen gardens which supplied the refectory. It lodged a community of one hundred twenty-five women made up of nuns, lay sisters, boarders, teachers and servants. Two men alone were granted entry, the priests who heard the confessions. The girls were allowed to leave its gates twice a month to visit relatives, but only during the daytime. Otherwise they were not permitted even a glimpse of the outside world, for every exterior window was barred and covered with heavy cloth.

But these bars, paradoxically, caused Aurore to experience a strange feeling of release. Her existence was cloistered, but she was at least no longer "torn apart—an apple of discord between two human beings whom I cherished." To be sure, she did not enjoy the physical discomforts. In the third-floor dormitory under the eaves which she shared with thirty girls, she lay shivering in her narrow bed at night, too cold to sleep. It was still dark at six o'clock in the morning when she and her classmates dressed, squeezing feet swollen with chilblains into their shoes. She had to break the ice in her basin to wash, then file down through stone passageways lit by flickering tapers to the dank chapel for Mass. Only afterward was she allowed to breakfast on dry bread and tea. Yet Aurore had no desire to escape. She felt so much at peace in her new surroundings that she did not even mind the gentle grilling she received on her first day of class.

Mother Alippe was in charge that day. She asked Aurore where the souls of children who had never been baptized went after death. Aurore had never received any religious education and did not have the least idea what the answer should be. Nevertheless she guessed that it was to the bosom of God.

"What are you saying, you wretched child?" cried Mother Alippe, outraged. "You obviously did not hear my question." Mother Alippe repeated it, then waited.

Aurore waited, too, for some other inspiration to strike her. In the silence, a classmate kindly whispered in her ear, "To Limbo . . ." but with such an English accent that Aurore mistook the word.

"To Olympus . . . ?" she said aloud in surprise. And she could not help laughing.

"For shame," cried Mother Alippe. "How dare you laugh during catechism!"

"Excuse me, Mother Alippe, I didn't do it on purpose."

"In that case I shall not require you to kiss the ground, but you must make the sign of the cross."

Unfortunately Aurore did not know how to do that either and touched her right shoulder before her left.

"Are you doing this on purpose, Miss?" retorted Mother Alippe, her outrage rekindling. She asked Aurore to repeat the gesture properly, but again Aurore did it the wrong way.

"Is that how you always do it?" demanded Mother Alippe.

"*Mon Dieu, oui* . . ." answered Aurore. "Dear Lord, yes . . ."

"*Mon Dieu!* You said *mon Dieu!* You are swearing."

"I . . . I don't think so."

"Oh, you unfortunate creature—where have you come from? You are a pagan—an absolute pagan!"

30

And for such transgressions Aurore was forced to wear a peaked nightcap all day as a punishment. But as she later wrote in her memoirs, "Religion at the convent seemed to me such a stupid and ridiculous affair that I resolved never to take it seriously."

She was pleased to discover that, of the three camps which existed among her classmates—the "goody-goodies," the "stupids" and the "devils"—it was the "devils" who recruited her. Throughout the first year and a half she followed them about and so heartily joined in their escapades that she earned the nickname "Madcap."

The "devils" went on secret excursions into the forbidden vaults and hidden passages of the convent in search of an imaginary "victim" supposedly buried alive some two hundred years before and still groaning to be let out. During one of these searches Aurore, scrambling over the rooftops, took a leap and toppled onto the roof tiles, losing a shoe. It fell with a rain of broken glass through a skylight into the hall outside the kitchen, but Aurore escaped with nothing more than bruised knees, for the destruction was blamed on one of the convent's cats. Other projects involved writing anonymous false confessions and leaving them about where they could be found by the shocked nuns. Still others were simple matters—hiding chicken bones in the piano or strewing slippery fruit peels in the dim corridors where the nuns passed on their way to prayers.

These diversions relieved the tedium of the long hours spent in chapel and in the classroom, where Aurore learned her catechism and "a little Italian, a little music, a little drawing . . . as little as possible if the truth be told." The only subject to which she applied herself seriously was English, for everyone around her spoke it and she did not want to be left out of convent life. She worked hard at her elementary spelling book and read *The Garden of the Soul*, while she practiced the language with Irish or English girls in her class.

There was a contagious fever among her friends to express themselves in literature, and Aurore was not immune. She began by writing poems, then moved on to novels. Her first novel, which stretched to a hundred pages, involved a pious hero called Fitz Gerald and an equally pious young girl whom he met in the country-side praying at a statue of the Madonna. Her friends pronounced it well-written but boring, and she did not even bother to show them her second effort, a novel of rural life. Finding it worse than the first, she used it, one cold winter night, to light her stove.

Aurore soon learned to speak English fluently and was transferred from the junior to the senior class, where she was given a cell of her own to live in. It was so tiny that she had to flatten herself against the man-sard window in order to close the door. Yet she managed to pack into it a wooden bed, an old chest of drawers, a straw-bottomed chair and her grand-mother's golden harp. Whenever she could, she used to escape to this "crumbling and wretched little niche" which she adored, for "only there did I belong to my-self. During the day I used to watch the clouds, the trees, the flight of the swallows. At night I would listen to the distant clamor of the big city melting into the country sounds from the suburbs." At daybreak the convent noises took over, with roosters crowing in the courtyard, chapel bells ringing for morning prayers, and the strident voice of Marie-Josèphe, the "waker-upper," going from room to room with a great grinding of door bolts as she emptied out the dormitories.

Aurore saw little of her mother, who paid rare visits to the convent and who "seemed to have accepted for herself a future of which I was no longer an essential part." She exchanged candid letters with her grandmother, knowing that the broad-minded woman would not mind her literary caricatures of some of the stricter nuns. But her grandmother lived most of the time at Nohant, and Aurore did not see her often. It was the custom for each girl at the convent, however, to choose from among the nuns and lay sisters an "adopted mother." Aurore found in the gentle veiled women about her a wide selection.

There was Sister Anne-Augustine, the old lady who mounted the stairs so slowly that, walking behind her, one could learn the day's lesson before reaching the top. There was Miss Hurst, who taught English and who had introduced Aurore to Shakespeare and Byron. There was a lean Scotswoman, Sister Teresa, who distilled mint liqueur in the cellar and often let Aurore help her. But the most beautiful and unreachable nun of all—outstanding for her goodness and tranquil piety— was Sister Alicia. She was not yet thirty and "her large blue eyes, bordered with black lashes, had a sweet, frank gaze. She was a generous soul, motherly and sincere." Aurore was determined to acquire her for her protector, and one day she told this to Sister Alicia.

"You . . . ? The worst devil in the convent?" the holy

sister responded, appalled. "What have I done that the Lord should inflict upon me the care of such a difficult child?"

"Give me a chance," Aurore pleaded. "Who knows? Maybe I'll reform just to please you."

"I should indeed be so fortunate!" answered Sister Alicia. "If I had any hope of improving you, I might resign myself to the task. But what a painful way to earn my salvation—I would have preferred any other! Can you at least promise to help me?"

"Not much," Aurore admitted. "I do not yet know who I am or what I can be. But I love you very much and I feel that, however I turn out, you'll be obliged to love me too."

"You certainly do not lack self-esteem," said Sister Alicia.

"Oh, it isn't that," Aurore replied. "But I need a mother. I have two who love me too much and whom I love too much, and all we do is hurt one another. It's hard for me to explain, and yet I think you understand. . . . Be a mother to me in your own fashion and I know I will adore that. Please, dear Mother, say yes. . . ."

Sister Alicia reluctantly assented. Every evening after the nuns, murmuring their prayers in Latin, had retired to their cells, Aurore would visit Sister Alicia's. There, among little religious keepsakes, among green vines trained over the cracks in the wall, Aurore would spend a precious quarter of an hour. She would talk of anything that came into her head—it didn't matter. What counted was having someone to confide in . . . someone to scold her gently, too, as Sister Alicia inevitably did, calling her her "torment."

34

It was not Sister Alicia, however, who was responsible for the sudden devoutness that overcame Aurore during her second year at the convent. It was rather that "I was fifteen years old and I needed an ardent passion. I needed to love something outside myself and I knew nothing on earth which I could love with all my strength."

With this mood upon her one evening, she found herself wandering listlessly through the paved cloisters—after hours and against regulations, as usual—wondering what to do. She toyed with the idea of some new prank. Should she put ink in the holy water? But that had been done already. Should she tie Mother Alippe's cat, Whisky, to the little cloister bell? But that had been done, too, often enough. Besides, she was bored with deviltry and wanted something else . . . but what?

As she was searching her mind, she saw the veiled nuns passing like furtive specters in the twilight on their way to the chapel to prostrate themselves before the altar. Curiosity (and the fact that this too was against the rules) caused her to follow quietly. Within, she beheld rococo columns, a stately organ, an altar covered with freshly cut jasmine. The white flame of a little silver lamp wavered in the shadows, illuminating marble floors, gilt frames, elaborately wrought candlesticks. A solitary star was captured in the stained-glass window. Aurore forgot the others. She was caught up by a new and unfamiliar sensation—a feeling of awe in her ready heart for God and a love for "this ideal of justice, tenderness and sanctity. . . . I saw a great road, immense, limitless, opening out before me; I burned to launch myself upon it."

35

Aurore was incapable of doing anything by halves. During the next months she "launched" herself into piety with a fervor and self-abnegation which dismayed the entire convent. The nuns were stunned to see her going without sleep, without food, and wearing a filigreed rosary which scratched her neck and drew blood. Her friends, the "devils," observing her face ever downcast in prayer, changed her nickname to "Saint Aurore." Aurore ignored them all. She had made up her mind that she would work toward becoming a lay sister like the humble servants of the convent who were crushed with backbreaking labor. She would take on only the lowliest jobs . . . sweeping the cellars, dragging out the pails of excrement, "having only God as witness to my tortures and His love alone for recompense."

She carried her devotions to such extremes that within a few months she fell dangerously ill. She suffered severe intestinal spasms and grew paler and weaker by the day. The Abbé de Prémord, a kind, fatherly priest, called her into the sacristy to see him.

"There is a measure of haughty pride concealed by this humility of yours," the perceptive old Jesuit observed. "Watch out—if you continue in this fashion, you will give piety a bad name. Who, with such a painful example as yours to contemplate, would be encouraged to embrace God . . . ?" He ordered her to return to the games and pleasures that suited her age and only on that condition would he grant her absolution.

Without abandoning her goal of joining the church, Aurore carried out the abbé's orders. Her return to the society of her friends was greeted like a resurrection. Since her conversion, there had not been one distinguished act of deviltry committed. Now, however, the activity of the "devils" took another form. Under Aurore's leadership, it was divested of its spirit of revolt and became a simple question of enjoying oneself, within the rules of the convent, to the fullest.

The girls improvised a theater, using a classroom which opened onto the garden as a stage. Costumes and sets were made from anything at hand. Two aprons sewn together became a man's cape, a ladder covered with a green carpet turned into a grassy bench. Aurore wrote short comic sketches and was the manager of the troupe, choosing the cast and ordering the costumes. As these sketches grew longer and more elaborate, news of the theater reached the ears of the convent authorities. The Mother Superior announced her desire that a whole evening be devoted to a four-hour spectacle which the entire convent community would attend.

Aurore felt the responsibility, for she had a new nickname now—"Author." The problem was how to make the nuns laugh without shocking them, for she did not want the theater to be closed down. It occurred to her that a Molière play she had read back in Nohant would fill the bill if she removed the love scenes. The works of Molière had been banned by the church because of his satirical jabs at the clergy. Because of this ban no nun had ever read Molière. It was impossible to obtain the forbidden text, but Aurore remembered a great deal of *Le Malade imaginaire* (*The Hypochondriac*).* When

---

*Titles in parentheses which are *italicized* are available in English translation.

it was put on that evening in an only slightly abridged form, it proved a tremendous success. The Mother Superior declared that she had never been so amused in all her life, while Aurore was covered with compliments. She whispered to her friends that she didn't deserve them—they belonged to Molière—her only merit was a good memory. The girls begged her to keep quiet for fear their theater would be suppressed.

The last six months Aurore spent at the convent "passed like a dream" . . . a dream she would have given anything to have extended into a lifetime. But her grandmother had grown concerned about her. The old freethinking lady, alarmed by the saintly tone of Aurore's letters, feared that her granddaughter was becoming *confite en Dieu*—pickled in God. More importantly, she was ailing and sensed she was approaching the end of her life. Before she died, she wanted to see Aurore married to an appropriate husband and thus removed from her mother's influence for good.

One day in April of 1820, Madame Dupin de Francueil came to take Aurore away from the convent. The girl hated to leave the community which she had come to consider "a paradise on earth" and where she was an adored figure to both nuns and pupils.

"I was frightened and desperate," she later wrote. " 'Do they want to marry me off?' I asked myself. Is it arranged already? Am I being taken out of the convent for that? Who then is this husband—this master—this enemy of all my desires and my hopes? Where is he hidden? How soon will my grandmother present him to me with the words, 'My child, you must say yes, or you will deal me a mortal blow!' "

But Aurore's two and a half years with the Dames Augustines Anglaises had taught her a great deal. The close study of the gospels had given her writing style a directness and simplicity which would mark it always. And she had also learned, from her months of intense religious fervor, that "devotion to an exalted idea has at least one strong effect upon a person's character—it kills self-love or, even if it only stuns it, helps to purge it of meanness and pettiness. . . ."

Aurore walked out the convent gates that spring day with a calm and contented air which concealed her fears from the frail old lady at her side.

3

With Aurore's return to the world at not quite sixteen, she immediately became an object of interest to matchmakers. An exchange of letters took place between a gentleman of the aristocracy and the Vicomtesse de Montlevic, a noblewoman friendly with Aurore's grandmother. The gentleman wrote:

Madame: You tell me that you know of an eligible young lady, a Mademoiselle Dupin, who—if I am not mistaken —is to come into an income of twenty to twenty-five thousand *livres*. My first cousin, Monsieur le Baron de Laborde, enjoys an income of eight to nine thousand *livres*. Though he is forty years old, there is nothing about him that a young girl would find physically repellent.

And the Vicomtesse de Montlevic replied:

Monsieur: Aurore is a brunette with a pretty figure and an agreeable face. In all she does she displays the manners of a person of the highest quality. The fortune, which she will inherit in the near future, is said to amount to some eighteen to twenty thousand *livres.*

Aurore, of course, had never laid eyes on the middle-aged baron in question. Nor did she know the army general—a man of fifty with a saber cut across his face—who also asked for her hand through an intermediary. Madame Dupin de Francueil refused both offers, although it was not the age of the gentlemen involved that troubled her. She simply felt that Aurore needed a few months—perhaps six months, even a year—before undertaking marriage.

Aurore spent two weeks in Paris before leaving for Nohant. She was relieved to learn of the reprieve she had been granted. Now she wanted to see her mother reconciled with her grandmother. But when she begged her mother to come back with them to the country, Sophie answered stubbornly that she would not set foot in Nohant again until her mother-in-law was dead. Aurore was pained by her mother's attitude but departed from her nonetheless in her grandmother's blue carriage.

Back once more at the beautiful country estate, she rejoiced at the clean open air and at a heady freedom whose taste she had almost forgotten. She put aside her drab uniform for the fresh gingham dresses a chambermaid brought her. She arranged her hair to suit herself without fear of someone's considering it indecent of her to leave her temples bare. She was delighted to discover her own room again, where workmen were covering the dingy orange walls with fresh lilac paint. Her treasured old bed, shaped like a hearse and sporting four now rather moth-eaten plumes at its corner posts, was still there. Enjoying the rare luxury of sleeping late, she lay listening to the nightingales in the woods and to the "distant, solemn, classical chant of the plowmen whose notes bore within them all the limpid and tranquil poetry of Berry."

Her half brother, Hippolyte, who was now sergeant of a cavalry regiment, arrived in Nohant for three months' leave. With his military swagger and his cap cocked jauntily over one ear, he seemed like a stranger at first, but soon he and Aurore picked up their old comradeship. Hippolyte was an expert horseman and Aurore begged him to teach her how to ride. "I do not know if I would have been afraid if I had thought about it," she later wrote, "but my brother didn't give me time." He brought out a horse called Colette which had not been broken in, gave its flanks a flick of his whip and sent Aurore off at a gallop.

"It was Hamlet's 'To be or not to be,'" Aurore recalled. "I concentrated all my will on not leaving that saddle. Five or six times I lost my seat and retrieved it, by the grace of God, and at the end of an hour—exhausted, disheveled and, above all, intoxicated—I grew confident." At the end of a week Aurore and Colette were leaping fences and fording streams, and "the quiet convent soul became bolder than a cavalryman and more robust than a peasant."

In the evenings everyone would gather in one of the downstairs rooms at Nohant where old furniture gleamed in the light of a crackling fire. Aurore would watch her grandmother and Deschartres bent over a game at the card table while she sat with a drawing pad, sketching. Sometimes she played the piano or read aloud. More often, she simply listened while her grandmother talked . . . about literature or music or the days of her youth when she had met the philosopher Jean-Jacques Rousseau. While she continued to correspond with her mother, Aurore grew ever fonder of the intelligent, sensitive old lady whose conversation she found "the best of books." And she was immensely grateful when her grandmother promised that she would never accept for Aurore any suitor with aristocratic prejudices which might cause him to reject Aurore's mother.

When her grandmother retired early, Aurore herself went to bed and read from ten in the evening till two or three o'clock in the morning. She came upon François René de Chateaubriand's *Genius of Christianity*, which condemned blind acceptance of religious dogma and encouraged a questing intellectual spirit. She felt released to enjoy the sort of literature which had been frowned upon at the convent, and she plunged into the philosophers and scientists. She discovered John Locke, Blaise Pascal, Aristotle, and Rousseau. Rousseau's doctrine of the absolute equality of men irrespective of their birth made a deep impression on her. Laying aside his *Social Contract*, she would take up her pen to set down notions of her own which she would later slip under her pillow . . . "Morally speaking, the

Just Man is of no particular sex; he is man or he is woman . . . whether a general in the army or the mother of a family, the code by which he lives is always the same."

Her former tutor, Deschartres, had not changed. He went about in his gray frock coat, outmoded breeches and white silk stockings, still grumbling in his kind-hearted but cantankerous old way. He never lost an opportunity to criticize Aurore's sketchy education at the convent or to upbraid her for her "crass igno-rance." And he was pleasantly surprised now when Aurore responded to his suggestion that she study a little surgery and anatomy. She had not lost her longing to devote herself to self-abnegating good works and was eager to accompany Deschartres on his visits to the sick and needy in Nohant. He had practiced medicine on the side for years, although he always refused to be paid for his services and flew into a rage if anyone dared thank him for them. Deschartres engaged a young med-ical student, Stéphane Ajasson de Grandsagne, who was spending the summer in nearby La Châtre, to give Aurore lessons. Stéphane came to Nohant frequently to teach Aurore science, and when she expressed an inter-est in osteology, he brought her a skeleton that she kept on her dressing table.

Aurore was an attractive young woman now with her flowing black hair, her supple figure, her sparkling dark eyes. At the end of the summer when Stéphane left for Paris, he wrote her letters which she suspected were love declarations, but she was so innocent that she could not really tell. She asked Deschartres for his opin-ion. The old pedagogue, innocent and unworldly in his own way, tried to puzzle out Stéphane's lofty and complex phrases, but could only come to the conclusion that they somehow expressed a note of despair . . . as indeed they had. Stéphane had fallen in love with his pupil, but knew he could not marry her. Even though Aurore would have infinitely preferred the handsome young medical student to her middle-aged suitors, neither Stéphane's family nor her grandmother would have ever agreed to such a match: Stéphane, though an unimpeachable aristocrat, was impoverished, and Aurore, though wealthy, was only half an aristocrat.

After Stéphane's departure, Aurore began to accompany Deschartres on his medical rounds. In the thatched huts of Nohant peasants who called Deschartres in any emergency, Aurore quickly learned to hold back her tears at the sight of blood or human suffering. Under Deschartres' instruction, she began to dress abscesses, help sew up wounds and even assist at amputations. At night she would sit by him in his room, so clean that it always smelled of lavender soap, while he taught her how to prepare medicines.

Though he would never admit it, the grumpy old tutor adored Aurore as he had adored her father. He found it undignified, however, always to be seen riding horseback alongside a female, and he tried to persuade Aurore that it was much easier to ride in a man's clothes. Aurore was tired of seeing "torn pieces of my embroidered petticoats hanging from every branch in the woods," tired "of the dresses then in vogue, so narrow that a woman was literally in a sheath and could not cross a brook with any decency without leaving a shoe behind her." She willingly took up Deschartres' suggestion; when she went on his rounds with him now, she put on a blue blouse, cap and trousers.

Since it was the custom in those days for men to wear their hair long, Aurore was occasionally taken for a man, but the conservative society of provincial La Châtre knew who she was and considered her behavior scandalous. No proper young woman, they insisted, would ride a horse unless it were sidesaddle on the croup behind her groom. Her men's clothes were an "abomination," her passion for the "bones of the dead" a profanity, her studies an "aberration." And when she was seen in the company of her childhood friends, who were the sons of her father's old friends in La Châtre, and "gave them a frank handshake without blushing or quivering like a young turkey in love," they found in her a brazenness which bordered on depravity, and said so on every possible occasion.

It was true that Aurore enjoyed a freedom unheard of for a young woman of her day. Her absent mother had not lost her daughter's affection, but she had lost all influence over her conduct. When Aurore received a sharp letter from Sophie criticizing her behavior, rumors of which had reached her in Paris, the girl replied, "I needed leading-strings when I was a child . . . but I am seventeen now and I know how to walk by myself." Her grandmother had suffered a stroke some nine months after their return to Nohant and was too feeble to leave her bed for more than short periods. Of necessity she had relinquished her authority over Aurore and their roles had reversed. The old lady became in a sense the child, worried over and cared for by the young girl, who became a kind of mother to her. Aurore took to sitting up all night in her grandmother's room, reading novels aloud to her restless and wakeful patient and giving her her medicines. The eccentric Deschartres, treating Aurore like the boy he wished she were, trained her in managing the estate and did his utmost to encourage her to be self-reliant and independent.

Approved of in her own home, it was easy for Aurore to ignore the wagging tongues of village gossips. Nor did she give any thought to the special significance of these days which only later she appreciated. "If it had been my destiny," she wrote, "to move straight from my grandmother's domination to the domination of a husband or of a convent, it is possible that I never would have turned into what I am. But when I was seventeen, the fates decided that I was to be free of all outside pressures, totally my own master for almost a year, and I became, for better or for worse, just about what I have been all the rest of my life."

Her unrestricted freedom came suddenly to an end, however, in late December of 1821, when Madame Dupin de Francueil died. Her last words were addressed to her granddaughter: "You are losing your best friend. . . ." Aurore, who had come to adore her grandmother, believed it to be so. But despite her grief, she felt she had no reason to dread the future. Madame Dupin de Francueil, before her death, had received Aurore's consent to bequeathing her guardianship to her noble cousin Count René de Villeneuve. He was a cultured man in his forties whom Aurore had met on one of his visits to Nohant. She had established a pleasant friendship with him. And when he arrived in Nohant, Aurore was prepared to leave with him for his beautiful Château de Chenonceaux whose vaulted arches bridged the river Cher. But Sophie Dupin turned up in Nohant for the reading of the will and complained bitterly. She called her late mother-in-law a woman with a "vicious heart." She refused to accept the clause which designated René de Villeneuve guardian and insisted upon her maternal rights.

Aurore was aware of the problems she might face living with her mother these days. Sophie Dupin was going through a difficult change of life and her volatile temperament gave way frequently to emotional and illogical outbursts. But Aurore was bound to her mother by ties of love and loyalty. When her patrician cousin made it clear that he and his wife, the Countess de Villeneuve, would refuse to have anything to do with her if she did not break with the "bird keeper" side of her family, Aurore packed her bags and followed Sophie to Paris.

They went to live in the comfortable apartment in the capital which had belonged to her grandmother. But "who could have said five years back that this reunion I had so desperately longed for would turn out to be sad and wretched?" George Sand later wrote. Sophie was fiercely jealous of the fine education which she had once wanted her daughter to enjoy; she took to snatching books from the girl's hand, claiming they were worthless. A servant Aurore was fond of and a dog she adored were the only precious associations she had not left behind at Nohant. Her mother sent them away without explanation. When Aurore asked to return for a while to the convent, her mother forbade her to go near it. Sophie Dupin's erratic moods began to border on the irrational. One day she would be kind and loving and would confide in Aurore, sadly admitting that she herself knew what an impossible person she was to live with. But the next day—or even a few hours later—she would turn into that "impossible" person again. Often it seemed as if Sophie could not make up her mind whether she really wanted to keep her daughter or to be rid of her by marrying her off.

Aurore herself had not given up hope of one day becoming a nun. "It is quite possible," she later wrote, "that I would have taken up that calling in three years' time, when I reached my majority, if my life had been bearable up till then. But it was becoming less and less so. . . ." It began to affect her nerves; she could neither eat nor sleep and she became subject to sudden and inexplicable bouts of fever. Tormented, she began to view marriage, which she had abhorred but a few months before, as the only conceivable escape from her mother's "autocratic rule."

When spring arrived, Sophie decided to take her daughter to spend a few days with friends of her late husband's. The Roëttiers du Plessis family, which lived near Melun not far from Paris, consisted of a warm, kindhearted couple and their five daughters. In their Louis XVI château, which echoed with the lively games and laughter of the young Roëttierses, Aurore was instantly made to feel at home. The very day after her arrival, however, one of Sophie's quixotic moods struck her. She returned to Paris alone, leaving Aurore to stay with the Roëttierses for many months. During that time, Aurore received several offers of marriage . . . not in person, to be sure, but as before through intermediaries. She refused them all because "I could not accept the idea of being sought in marriage by men who did not know me, who had never seen me, and who consequently only considered me a good bargain."

One day when the Roëttierses took Aurore to the theater in Paris and went afterward to eat ice cream at a popular café in the capital, a lieutenant in the French army came over to their table. He was a friend of the Roëttierses' called Casimir Dudevant. "A thin young man, rather elegant, with a cheerful face and a military bearing," the twenty-seven-year-old Casimir was the illegitimate though acknowledged son of Baron Dudevant, a former officer who had retired to his estate in Gascony. Aurore observed that Casimir had more the frank openness of a soldier than the mannered ways of an aristocrat. After being introduced to Aurore, he immediately asked Madame Roëttiers in a low voice who she was. The motherly woman was very fond of Aurore and jokingly replied, "My daughter." "She is to be my wife then?" Casimir joked back, for Madame Roëttiers had once promised him he should marry one of her many girls. "If you will grant me her hand, I accept!" Madame Roëttiers began to laugh but, as George Sand later wrote, "the joke was a prophecy."

During the coming weeks Casimir made frequent visits to the Roëttierses in the country. Aurore liked the wholehearted way the young lieutenant joined in the spirited games she organized for the Roëttiers girls, and the two became congenial companions. Before long Casimir decided that he really did want to marry Aurore. He made no ardent advances, however, no romantic speeches to her—it was not in his character. One

49

day he simply said to her, "This is not the way such things are usually done, perhaps, but I wanted you to give me your consent yourself, without any outside pressure. If you feel no antipathy toward me and if you can't decide right now, study me a little more during the next few days and then tell me whether you would like me to authorize my father to speak to your mother."

Strangely, the almost matter-of-fact way Casimir approached Aurore proved the most effective way of pleading his cause. She was emerging from "a period of terrible conflict, torn between family and church—a sudden passion at that time would have frightened me." She admired Casimir for his honesty and his goodness, for the frank friendship he offered her which had nothing of the fortune hunter in it. And she gave him her consent.

But Aurore could not marry without her mother's consent as well. For some time Sophie hesitated, saying yes one day and no the next. Casimir, though manly and distinguished, was not handsome, and Sophie pretended to object to the length of his nose. But in the end she gave in. On September 17, 1822, Aurore and Casimir Dudevant were married in Paris at the church of Saint-Louis d'Antin. Shortly afterward the eighteen-year-old bride arrived with her husband in Nohant, where they were joyfully welcomed by old Deschartres and where they settled down to live.

Aurore was determined to make her marriage a happy one. "It is absolutely necessary," she wrote a girl friend from her convent days, "for one of the partners in a marriage to give way totally to the other and to renounce not only all personal wishes but even all personal opinions. The only thing that remains to be decided is which one should *change* to fit the other, the man or the woman? Since the bearded half of the human race is all-powerful, it is obviously we women who must bow down in obedience."

She tried to follow her own precepts. When she lay in the ornate plumed bed with Casimir and he treated his virginal wife with an insensitivity which made the act of love seem brutal and repellent, she hid her unhappiness and submitted in silence. Casimir was not unkind, but he had a soldier's way with women.

When Casimir took her authority away from her in the running of the estate, she submitted too, without a word. She was no longer mistress of Nohant except in name, in any case. With her marriage, her fortune and property had fallen under her husband's control and she was left with only a small allowance for her personal needs.

Even when Casimir began to destroy the precious scenes of her childhood—as he transformed the lovely wilderness of the gardens at Nohant into well-ordered paths, trimmed hedges and neat alleyways—Aurore told her husband she approved. In fact, in her eagerness to be a good wife, Aurore told Casimir that she approved of everything he did, yet "I was troubled and even though I could find nothing in my conscious mind that I could point to as bad, I felt crushed by a new and sick repugnance for life."

To escape her troubled mood, she plunged into domesticity. She began to knit and, soon, to sew for the baby she was expecting. She discovered she took the same pleasure her mother did in working cleverly with a needle, and sometimes she displaced the cook at Nohant to produce a batch of currant preserves. Within a year of her marriage she gave birth to a son she named for her father and great-grandfather—Maurice. She had always loved children and had been a favorite with the younger girls at the convent. Now she laid aside her intellectual pursuits while she nursed and cared for little Maurice, feeding him herself and watching over him devotedly.

But when Maurice had been weaned and her brief period of exclusive domesticity had passed, Aurore began once more to feel a passion for books, for music and for the absorbing philosophical talks which she had carried on before with Deschartres. Her old tutor was gone. He had decided that two managers were one too many for Nohant and had retired to Paris. Afterward he died there obscurely, without notifying a soul that he had even been ill. Aurore's half brother, Hippolyte, had married and was living near Nohant, but he reacted to rural idleness by drowning his boredom in alcohol and was often inarticulate. Most of all, Aurore longed for spiritual companionship with her husband. Casimir, however, was no reader. He preferred to spend his days hunting. The music his wife loved to play on the new piano he had bought her was simply noise that tortured his eardrums. And whenever it came to embarking upon a subject more complex or elevating than workaday matters, Casimir fell asleep in his chair.

Casimir considered his wife's persistent desire for intellectual discussions with him to be merely the result of "overexcited nerves," "a bilious temperament"; and he ignored it. He felt more at ease with Hippolyte, with whom he swapped army jokes during long evenings over the bottle. When the two men were drunk, Aurore would escape to a little room she had made her own on the ground floor, where she would read or try to write. But she left her efforts unfinished, for she found them discouragingly inept.

When Casimir and she dined at the homes of their neighbors in La Châtre, Aurore found she had little to say. While the men withdrew to talk politics, she was left with the women who talked about clothes or exchanged gossip, and she was interested in neither. She preferred playing with the children, as she had done at the Roëttierses', to listening to drawing-room conversation. Or she simply liked to sit and dream "of some imaginary oasis mean or idle people were never tempted to enter." Her alternating moods of gaiety and dreaminess made people consider her very strange, while Casimir judged her "idiotic." "Little by little he made me feel the superiority of his reasoning and intelligence until I sat crushed and stupid in other people's company."

One morning at the breakfast table, during the second year of her marriage, Aurore was suddenly "suffocated by tears." Her husband was astonished. She could not produce any good reason for them. She told Casimir that she had had similar moods before. She suggested they were perhaps due to her "weak and disturbed brain." Casimir could only agree with her, and he proposed a change of air.

He and Aurore began to travel. They spent the spring months with the Roëttierses in Melun. Their friends' château, where Casimir Dudevant had proposed to Aurore, was filled as before with young people. Aurore joined in the amateur theatricals and community games with rediscovered energy that often knew no limits. One day when she and some teenage girls were tossing sand at each other, while the gentlemen and older ladies took their coffee in the parlor overlooking the gravel terrace, a few grains of sand fell into Casimir's cup. He sprang to his feet angrily and ordered Aurore to stop or he would slap her. "I don't believe it!" she flung back at him, laughing, and kept up her game. With the others looking on, Casimir struck his wife a stinging blow across the face. She proudly hid her humiliation and ran off with the young girls into the garden, where she wept furious tears. Years later it seemed to her that "this brief but significant incident altered forever my confidence in Monsieur Dudevant's character." At the time, however, she did her best to put it out of her mind.

In the autumn, after leaving the Roëttierses, she and Casimir took a house in Ormesson, not far from Paris, where other friends joined them. Aurore passed her days in the garden reading the essays of Michel de Montaigne while little Maurice played at her feet. Later they moved into an apartment in Paris, where still other friends, old and new, came to pass social evenings. For a while Aurore recovered her spirits, yet "a nameless sadness" would come over her from time to time. And when she and Casimir returned to Nohant, she felt more than ever that "the present was empty, the future frightening."

In July of 1825, when she turned twenty-one, Aurore

and Casimir again left to travel southward to the Pyrenees mountains. The pretext was Aurore's health—she was thought to be consumptive—but in reality she and Casimir had begun to dread "finding ourselves face to face, with different instincts in every regard and with characters which had nothing in common. We had no desire to hide anything from each other, it was simply that we did not know how to talk to each other." She and Casimir never argued. Aurore was still trying to see everything through her husband's eyes, "to think and to act according to his desires. But the moment I managed to agree with him, I found myself disagreeing with my own instincts and I grew desolate."

In the Pyrenees, Casimir and Aurore joined friends at a mountain resort, where they began to explore the surrounding area. Taking off on her horse in the morning, Aurore galloped through the mists of tumbling waterfalls and along the edges of precipices. Leaving the others far behind, she braved steep paths and perilous descents. At nightfall, she changed her exhausted mount which "had not allowed me to break my neck, though I did all I could to do so," and rode back through the darkness after sometimes covering thirty-six leagues in one day. The next morning she rode off again.

Her husband grumbled that she was "making herself conspicuous." One of her women friends took her aside and scolded her for her strange moods . . . for the way she broke into laughter at times over nothing, for the way she galloped away like a wild woman at the risk of her life. Aurore answered distraughtly that her friend didn't understand; sometimes a person needed to black everything out, needed to forget.

"Forget what?" returned the puzzled friend.

"How should I know? Forget everything . . . above all forget that I exist!"

Alone in her hotel room at night, Aurore began to keep a diary. She knew now that her marriage was a mismatch—as distressing to Casimir perhaps as it was to her—and yet the law had bound them together for as long as they lived. In an attempt to adjust herself to this reality, she wrote one day, "I cried a great deal during my walk, but what is the point of tears? You must keep a smile on your face even though you feel something dying in your soul." In a marriage like hers she saw no "middle course" for someone who was neither a saint nor an unfeeling dolt, though she added, "Yes, there is a middle course after all—it is despair."

At the resort Aurore met a lawyer from Bordeaux, Aurélien de Sèze, who was vacationing with his fiancée and her family. The twenty-six-year-old Aurélien soon forgot his fiancée, however. He was enthralled by Aurore's dark, beautiful eyes and by the melancholy soul beneath her vivacious exterior. He was struck, too, by the mind of this unusual young woman.

Aurélien was everything Casimir was not—handsome, sensitive, poetic. While Casimir was off hunting chamois or shooting eagles, Aurore took long walks with Aurélien. They talked about literature and philosophy, and Aurore found in Aurélien the intellectual companion she had sought in her husband. She felt she had come upon a twin soul. Her loyalty to Casimir, however, and the respect which she and Aurélien felt for the sanctity of marriage, caused them to make a painful decision: Though they would cherish each other always, they would never go beyond the bounds of platonic friendship.

For years afterward—and with Casimir's knowledge—they carried on a correspondence which kept the postal service busy between Bordeaux and Nohant. They wrote each other about politics, about poetry, about everything that happened in their lives, but mentioned their love for one another only in the purest of terms. In the end, of course, that love could not survive geography and lack of personal contact. Yet the episode left its impression on Aurore.

One day in late fall of 1825, she sat down and composed a long letter to Casimir. In it she bared her heart to her husband and wrote of her deep unhappiness over their marriage. She spoke of her yearnings for the intimate "communion of souls" which might have made it beautiful but which, with unintentional cruelty, he had consistently rejected. "Whenever we discussed works of literature, of poetry or of ethics, you had not read the authors and you treated my thoughts as if they were the mad excesses of a romantic mind. I gave up talking about them. . . ." She hastened to insist that Casimir had always been generous and good to her and that if he had been the cause of her wretchedness, he had been so without realizing it. Covering twenty pages, she included an account of her friendship with Aurélien. But it was not to destroy their marriage that she was writing Casimir; it was with the hope of joining with him to make it what a marriage should be. She set down a series of articles which she begged him to think over. . . .

Article 3: If we spend the winter in Paris, we will study languages together. You will improve your learning and share my intellectual interests and it will give me the greatest pleasure imaginable. While I sketch or do needlework, you will read aloud, and our days will flow by in a delightful manner. Please note that I do not ask you to love music; I will bore you with it as little as possible and only play the piano when you are out walking.

Article 5: If we spend the winter in Nohant, we will read many of the worthwhile books in the library there and with which you are not acquainted. We will discuss them. You will give me your impressions, I will give you mine. All our ideas, all our pleasures, will be shared in common.

Article 7: Banishing all bitter thoughts or regrets, we shall be happy and at peace. Side by side, we shall strive toward perfection.

Casimir responded to the letter by getting drunk with Hippolyte, yet at the same time its contents had an effect upon him which he could not shake off. He resolved to give up hunting and shooting. He took a book from the library and attempted to read it. When he went off on trips, he would return with more books or an English dictionary . . . and he assured his wife that he would no longer spend his life aimlessly but would pass it profitably at her side.

He labored at self-improvement. But the "laziness" which he told Aurore had prevented him in the past from "reading what, so far as I can tell, elevates the soul and teaches a man to think and to reason" took possession of him once again. Finding the task he had set himself beyond his powers and his inclinations, he soon gave it up. The "articles" were mentioned no more.

Casimir turned back to his old occupations, hunting

or drinking with Hippolyte, and to a new occupation now, too. In September of 1828, when Aurore was resting in bed after the birth of her second child, a daughter, Solange, she could hear muffled talk in the next room between Casimir and a servant girl, Pepita, which revealed his intimate relations with the girl. Before long she learned that this was only one of several affairs which her husband was carrying on. As time passed, he made no attempt to conceal them from her.

Aurore was forced to adjust to the utter failure of her married life. She put up a hammock in her tiny study and made it her bedroom. She continued to live in the same house with Casimir—she had no alternative. Her husband had lost a great deal of her money in rash business speculations, but he maintained control now even over the small personal allowance, which she had relinquished to help make up for debts. Yet while she bore her "slavish position" with an outwardly composed air, she resented it. She was in her mid-twenties now, with a growing need to feel "that I was a person who existed in my own right."

She tried to strike out on her own whenever she could. In summer, she renewed old friendships with the young men of La Châtre whom she had known in her teens. There was the towering and burly Alphonse Fleury, nicknamed "The Gaul" because of his flowing mustache. There was the rich "milord" Gustave Papet, fair-haired Charles Duvernet, and frail and poetic Jules Sandeau. Leaving Casimir to his amorous adventures, Aurore mounted Colette in the morning and rode away from Nohant to join her friends, who were spending their holidays in each other's company. They always

Aurore and Casimir
Dudevant.
Painting by
François Biard.

Maurice and Solange.
Drawing by
Nancy Mérienne.

welcomed her at Charles Duvernet's château, where they gathered. She spent long hours with them arguing over philosophy, politics or literature, while they lounged on the grass in the shade of gnarled old pear trees.

Students at universities in Paris, these young intellectuals brought to the countryside the rebellious ideas of the Romantic Movement then in vogue. Bourgeois middle-class morality with its hidebound restrictions was, they held, stodgy and outdated and deserved to be trampled underfoot. Total freedom must reign instead. They believed in freedom for the oppressed masses whose revolutionary causes they supported. But even more important in their eyes was individual freedom— which they elevated to a new morality. Whatever the heart desired, they insisted, was natural—in harmony with human nature—and therefore "right." The rules and restrictions society imposed on the individual were artificial—against nature—and therefore "wrong."

Aurore found it easy to accept their way of thinking. She had long admired Rousseau's writings, which were the inspiration for this Romantic Movement. Moreover, the sanctity of her marriage, which she had been so careful to preserve during her platonic friendship with Aurélien de Sèze, had been turned into a mockery by Casimir's blatant promiscuity with other women. She saw no reason now why she should be—unilaterally— the victim of "bourgeois conventions." And when one of the young men in the group, Jules Sandeau, fell in love with her, no further scruples prevented her from meeting the golden-haired young man in the woods or in the little garden house at Nohant.

61

When winter came, however, the "Berrichons," as she called them—for they were almost all natives of the province of Berry—returned to Paris. She kept up a correspondence with them, but this was no substitute for their presence and she grew despondent. There was another reason as well for her despondency. These young men were studying law or medicine and soon would be pursuing purposeful careers in the world. She could see no such future for herself.

"I suffered terribly at the sight of my own useless-ness," she wrote, and she picked up the work she had once shared with Deschartres—doctoring and helping the poor. She passed entire days galloping on Colette from one farmhouse to another. "I mend broken noses," she wrote her mother, "stitch up cut fingers, concoct potions for colds, make poultices. . . ." She gave herself entirely to this voluntary labor. Before long she was able to pass a peasant dwelling where a family was sitting contentedly under a roof that no longer leaked and say to herself that it was she "who had repaired that house, protected those children from smallpox and [healed] that son who had almost died in the field during the harvest."

The satisfaction this work brought her seemed at times a compensation for her emotional loneliness. But at other times she was overwhelmed by the barrenness of life at Nohant. She longed to be in faraway Paris, convinced "that beyond the limits of my life there ex-isted a rare and enlightened society where gifted people met to exchange their feelings and ideas. My imagina-tion lured me on toward this world. . . . I would have walked ten leagues to see Monsieur Balzac pass by."

Yet at Nohant, where "each day resembled the next," Aurore might read a book by Honoré de Balzac, but he certainly did not pass by the curtained window of her study. No one did except the creatures of her own invention as she tried to set down the beginnings of a novel. She wrote without any intention of becoming a writer, but just to fill the empty hours when Solange was taking naps or Maurice having lessons with a tutor. Her only companion was a little cricket who sat on her sealing wax. Sometimes he would walk over her page and she would chase him off for fear he would poison himself with the fresh ink. Glancing up one day she saw that a servant had closed the window and crushed him. As she sadly buried his remains in the white petals of a trumpet lily, she "could not describe the impression this childish incident made upon me. I kept thinking, in spite of myself, that the voice of a cricket—which is truly the voice of the domestic hearth—could have sung my real happiness. At least it might have murmured a lullaby over the last glow of that sweet illusion which it had now flown off with forever. The death of the cricket marked, like a symbol, the end of my stay at Nohant."

One day she walked into Casimir's study and found an envelope addressed to her, but bearing the inscription: NOT TO BE OPENED UNTIL AFTER MY DEATH. Aurore decided to open it all the same. "Great God! What a testament!" she later wrote a friend. "Nothing but curses. He put into it all his irritation, all his anger, all his feelings of contempt for my character. I thought that I must be dreaming. Indeed, till that moment I had kept my eyes tightly shut because I did not want to see that contempt. Now his words awakened me at last."

The cupboard which folded down to make a desk in Aurore's study at Nohant.

The same day Aurore went to Casimir. She announced that she was going to Paris to make her own living. When she succeeded, she would send for Solange, while Maurice would remain temporarily in the care of his tutor. She planned to spend six months of every year at Nohant, she explained, but she asked Casimir for an allowance which would permit her to live the other six months alone in the capital.

Casimir listened in disbelief to his wife who spoke "with a poise and coolness which stunned him. He had hardly expected someone like me to rise to my feet and face up to him." When she had finished, "he scolded, he argued, he pleaded," but Aurore—revealing some of the iron of her great-grandfather, the Count de Saxe—clung to her decision. When Casimir saw that nothing would change her mind and that she was at least willing to keep up the surface appearances of their marriage, he wept but he gave in to her.

On January 4, 1831, Aurore packed her trunks and made ready to take the coach for Paris. Hippolyte thoroughly disapproved of his sister's behavior, and before her departure, he tried to shame her out of it.

"Don't tell me you really think you can live in Paris on two hundred fifty francs a month," he snorted. "The idea is ridiculous! *You . . . ?* Why, you don't even know the price of a chicken—you'll come back in a fortnight without a penny in your pocket!"

"Perhaps," Aurore answered. "But I am going to try."

4

At 31 rue de Seine in Paris stood a four-story building with mansard windows peering down upon a narrow street of market carts and rattling carriages. To one side, a few blocks away, was the University of the Sorbonne in the Latin Quarter, where cobblestoned boulevards and sidewalk cafés were thronged with long-haired students in top hats and flapping redingotes. To the other side, the gray-green river Seine flowed under stone bridges where "slate-colored pigeons made their nests." Hippolyte kept an empty apartment in this building for his occasional visits to Paris, and Aurore moved into it when she arrived in the capital to begin "a new phase of my life."

She was twenty-six years old and unaware of just how ill-equipped for this she was. "I had many fixed ideas on abstract matters," she later recalled, "but I was totally ignorant of reality." When she had told Casimir that she planned to make her own living, she had had no notion of how to do so. She still did not have one now as she counted out the pitifully few coins in her purse, tried to plan a budget, and came to the realization that she would not have enough money from her allowance even to pay for logs in the fireplace. Yet, for all this, the ideal of the Romantics had become her own and she rejoiced in a personal liberty which she considered her "legitimate right."

"I had kept this ideal of mine closed up in a hidden

corner of my brain and it took no more than a few days of utter freedom to make it burst into bloom. I carried it with me as I roamed the icy streets, my shoulders covered with snow, my hands in my pockets. Sometimes my stomach was empty but my head was perhaps all the fuller for that, stirring with dreams and melodies, colors and shapes, marvelous and mysterious visions."

She went one day to visit her old convent. None of her former classmates were there anymore, and the nuns she found vague, preoccupied with their own closed religious world. She left the iron gates behind her without any regrets this time. She paid visits, as well, to the school friends she had occasionally corresponded with over the years. She discovered "these young heiresses had become countesses now and were more orthodox than ever in their ideas. I returned without a grain of sadness to my mansard room and my utopia."

Paris was in ferment all around her during her first winter there in 1831. The previous July, students, shopkeepers and workers in the capital had taken up arms. Unwilling to be dominated any longer by a small feudal aristocracy, they had overthrown the monarchy of Charles X. They had intended to set up a republic—a state governed by representatives democratically elected by the people. The "republicans," as they were called, had almost succeeded, but the powerful bourgeoisie managed to crush the popular rebellion and place another monarch on the throne. This new "bourgeois king," Louis-Philippe, walked the streets wearing a business suit and carrying a black umbrella. Yet he represented only a new kind of oppressive rule in the

Paris in the 1830's. Painting by Giuseppe Canella.

eyes of the republicans—the rule of rich industrialists. As before, the vast majority of people—impoverished workers and peasants—were denied democratic rights. And so now the republicans were forming revolutionary groups to challenge the new government.

Artists and intellectuals of the day were no less stirred. The followers of the philosophy of Claude Henri de Saint-Simon, who proclaimed the equality of all men, were meeting in clubs in various parts of the city. Victor Hugo's *Hunchback of Notre Dame* was shocking literary critics by its anticlericalism in portraying a Catholic priest inflamed by sexual desire. A controversy that arose when the great actress Marie Dorval performed in a play which condoned adultery and illegitimacy added to the general tumult. Aurore longed to be witness to it all, the way her Berrichon friends were.

Most of these young men from her summer in Berry were in the capital now—the bewhiskered "Gaul" Alphonse Fleury, Jules Sandeau with his mass of golden curls "like a little Saint John the Baptist," the rich "milord" Gustave Papet who usually picked up the restaurant checks. And there were others—a law student, Félix Pyat, and a medical student, Émile Regnault—who joined the group which formed a Berrichon Club in Paris.

Aurore wanted to accompany them to political street meetings, and to student restaurants and to their artists' haunts in the Latin Quarter, but "respectable" women were simply not seen in such places. No woman went out with a band of unattached young men without risking being branded a prostitute. Aurore thirsted to go to the theater with them, but they bought the cheapest seats in the pit, which were all she could afford and where only men sat. Women were obliged to sit with fitting escorts or chaperons in the expensive dress circle or in the boxes. As Balzac wrote, "You can't be a woman in Paris unless you have an income of at least twenty-five thousand francs a year."

Since her marriage Aurore had become only too familiar with the legal restrictions imposed on women by the Napoleonic Code, which was still the law of the land. Regarding a woman "a minor even at eighty," the Code deprived her of control over her property, over her children's education, of a voice in deciding where she could live or whom she could see. She knew only too well that a man could commit adultery and not suffer any consequences, while a woman could be sent to prison for the same offense; a man could even go unpunished for the murder of an unfaithful wife.

Now she was confronted in Paris with an equally harsh moral code, for all that it was not written down in any book of law. It forbade her freedom of movement to widen her intellectual horizons, and she was "cut off for good" from her men friends who, she wrote enviously, "were seeing everything, going everywhere." Soon she could not even go out into the streets because her "fine shoes wore out after two days on the paving stones. My little velvet hats, my dresses, bespattered with mud from the gutters, went to ruin with an alarming rapidity." And she had no money with which to replace them.

Aurore saw only one solution. Recalling the old days with Deschartres when she had worn boys' clothes for their rides through the woods, she decided to disguise herself as a man. Without giving any particular thought to what others might think, she had herself fitted for a gray redingote with trousers and vest to match. She added to this a gray top hat, a thick woolen scarf and a pair of sturdy boots with metal-tipped heels. There remained only the problem of her voice . . . which she lowered to "a muted, deep pitch." Whenever she wished to, now, she could be "the perfect replica of a first-year student."

Waiters at Chez Pinson, the Left Bank restaurant where her friends from Berry gathered to argue the issues of the day, addressed her unwittingly as "Sir." When a lady dropped her bouquet at the Théâtre-Français and Aurore did not think to pick it up, she heard the woman comment curtly on the shocking lack of chivalry in modern young men. Everyone Aurore met was taken in by her disguise, and she was delighted. She could go wherever she chose—leave the house at any hour, return at any hour—without exciting the slightest comment. She could brave all weather in her new clothes, and they allowed her such freedom of movement that she "flew from one end of Paris to the other, feeling as if I could go right on around the world." Her Berrichon friends were no less delighted. Eccentricity of dress, which flouted rigid convention, was part of the creed of the Romantics. Then, too, it was a rare pleasure for them to talk to a woman on the same intellectual plane as their own and to take her with them wherever they went.

Before long nearly all of these young Berrichons were more or less in love with Aurore. She was smitten with only one of them, however, the gold-haired young man she had met secretly in the woods at Nohant—Jules Sandeau. Something maternal in her was touched by the frailty of this aspiring writer seven years her junior. His pallor, moreover, which gave him the air of someone trailing a faint illness, was held attractive by the young Romantics who, as part of their poetic pose, often forced themselves to look or even actually become sickly.

Aurore confined her relations with Casimir to friendly but brief letters to Nohant, yet she sorely missed her children. In order not to be separated from them for too long, she planned to divide her six months in Paris into two periods of three months each. She had very little time, therefore, to prove to Casimir and Hippolyte—and, above all, to herself—that she was capable of making her own living.

The possibilities open to Aurore were limited, since women were not accepted in universities and were thus unqualified to work in professions such as law or medicine or politics. She was clever with a paintbrush, however. At Nohant she used to decorate snuffboxes and cigar cases with tiny birds and flowers, and she thought of trying to sell such objects now. She soon discovered that the fashion for them had passed. When she painted a portrait of her doorkeeper, she was encouraged by a café proprietor who offered to hang it for her. Unfortunately, no one came in to buy it. Aurore then dipped into her trunk and took out a novel she had written at Nohant. Recently she had discovered she could write "quickly, easily and for long hours without tiring." But when it occurred to her that she might turn her pastime

Jules Sandeau.
Sketch by George Sand.

Two strollers. The person
on the right is said to be
George Sand. By Gavarni.

into a profession, she was troubled by doubts. "Did I have any talent? Or was I merely mistaking my inclination for real ability? I felt I had to know. . . ."

She went to see Hyacinthe de Latouche, editor of the newspaper *Figaro.* A brilliant man with a scathing tongue, Latouche received Aurore cordially. Her father had been one of his father's friends and he himself came from her own province of Berry. But when he had glanced over a few pages of the novel she showed him, he asked her if she had any children. She told him she had, though she could not afford yet to keep them with her. Did she really intend then to live in Paris and make a living by her pen? She responded that she was obliged to. Latouche declared that he saw nothing in her work which showed the slightest promise; it was, in a word, "abominable." He advised her to return to her home and her husband.

Aurore listened to Latouche respectfully but was reluctant to take his advice. Instead she sought out François Duris-Dufresne, a governmental representative from the province of Berry and a friend of hers and Casimir's. The liberal statesman was well disposed toward Aurore, whose mind he had always admired. When she asked him to introduce her to someone else who could give her a professional opinion, he suggested the novelist Auguste de Kératry.

At eight o'clock the next morning, Aurore presented herself, eyes swollen with sleep, at Monsieur de Kératry's door. She was wearing a dress that day, as she often did when there was no reason to don her man's disguise. The white-haired author ushered her in and, without any preamble, announced, "Monsieur Duris-

74

Dufresne has informed me that you wish to write. I promised him to speak to you about this project of yours. I will not waste words. I shall be utterly frank. A woman has no business writing."

"If that is all you have to say to me," Aurore answered, "it was hardly worth rousing me at such an hour." And she started from the room.

But Monsieur de Kératry followed her into the vestibule. There he continued to develop his theory of the inferiority of women and the impossibility of even the most intelligent of them producing anything of value. Aurore tried to escape from his harangue, but even as she was going out the door, Kératry held her back to insist, "You will do well to take my advice—don't make books, make children!"

Everywhere she went in search of work or counsel, she met with similar rebuffs. She did not even attempt to approach some editors personally . . . Louis Véron, for instance, the editor-in-chief of the *Revue de Paris*, who "detests women and won't hear the subject mentioned." Instead she had a friend submit to him an article on which she and Jules Sandeau had collaborated and to which Sandeau alone had put his name. But now she found that being a woman, though an immense obstacle, was not the only one which stood in her way. The *Revue de Paris* returned the article without giving it a reading because "it was the work of an unknown writer and therefore could not possibly have any merit."

Closed up in her Paris garret, and filling page after page of notepaper, Aurore continued to apply herself to writing. "It is leading me nowhere as yet, though I bury myself in it and work like a dog." She was not after glory; her only desire was to "earn a little money." And sometimes she admitted that "if I had foreseen half the problems which I am encountering, I never would have undertaken this career. Still I am always hopeful, and then a strange thing is happening to me . . . the more obstacles I face, the more difficulties I see in my path, the greater is my ambition to overcome them."

Latouche, the editor of the *Figaro*, had kept in touch with Aurore after their first interview. Seeing his determined young Berrichon compatriot working and struggling and becoming only the poorer for it, he felt moved, despite his misgivings about her abilities, to offer her a small job on his newspaper. The pay was poor, the work inconsequential, but it was an opportunity not only to earn some money at last, but to improve her writing under professional guidance. Aurore accepted gratefully.

The *Figaro* in those days was a satirical paper of republican tendencies which produced pinpricking articles against the government of King Louis-Philippe. Latouche made up the issues himself, working with a group of "young eagles" who wrote under his direction and whose company Aurore joined. She and her colleagues would sit scribbling at small tables arranged around the fireplace in his drawing room, while Latouche strode up and down, spurring them on with caustic comments and criticisms.

Though she tried hard to keep pace with the others, Aurore failed hopelessly. Latouche would suggest a topic and ask her to write an article about it in one page. Before she knew it, she would have covered ten messy pages which had barely touched on the subject, and she would be forced to throw them all into the fire. At the end of the first month, she had produced so little that she received only fifteen francs for her efforts, and even that she considered a gross overpayment. But gradually she began to acquire the habit of writing more concisely and in the humorous and satirical manner which characterized the *Figaro*'s style.

One day, in the second month of her job, she wrote a piece which, though anonymous (as was everything she wrote for the *Figaro*), brought its author unexpected notoriety. Because of King Louis-Philippe's fear of new uprisings, his government had taken severe restrictive measures against freedom of assembly. Aurore described these measures in an article which ended with the mock announcement: "Every Monday, Wednesday and Friday shall henceforth be devoted to forbidding meetings and every Tuesday, Thursday and Saturday to breaking them up."

Parisian readers were delighted with her piece, which was couched throughout in the same taunting vein. The King, however, was furious and sent out immediate orders to his Prefect of Police. This issue of the *Figaro* was impounded, but Aurore's anonymity was not uncovered and further legal proceedings were called off. The furor aroused by her satirical piece constituted a minor triumph for Aurore. She could now consider herself to be, in her own small way, a professional writer. She soon set about writing articles for other papers with Jules Sandeau, who continued to lend her the shelter of his name.

When Aurore was not working at Latouche's, she was

working in her mansard room at home. Sometimes she would shove her papers aside to run off with Jules to the Latin Quarter, or to attend a new performance at the Opéra, where she heard the first concert in Paris of the phenomenal violin virtuoso Niccolò Paganini. Sometimes she would disguise herself as a man and sit in at a stormy session of the legislative assembly to listen to the Marquis de Lafayette—the hoary-headed French hero of the American War of Independence—engage in debate. Or she would be caught up in a street riot of anticlericalists who were demolishing churches, while drums calling out the king's soldiers beat the night through. Rushing to see as much of Paris life as she could, she scarcely had time to give thought to the fact that she was the only woman working as a journalist in all of France. In any case, she preferred to keep her identity hidden, not only for professional reasons, but because she did not want to upset her relatives.

In a letter to Sophie Dupin, who was staying in the country with Caroline at the time, Aurore wrote: "You ask me what I am doing here in Paris. Oh, what everyone else in Paris does, I suppose—just amusing myself. I go to museums, to the theater, I take drawing lessons . . . and all this keeps me so busy that I really don't see a soul."

Significantly enough, however, though she hid it from her family, she did not seek to hide from anyone else her liaison with Jules Sandeau. She was not ashamed of it. She did not consider her behavior in any way incorrect. On the contrary, "when the heart speaks, it is always right," she insisted, and she was proud to follow its dictates. Whenever the Berrichons gathered on misty Paris evenings in someone's cramped dwelling, she was there, and with her always was Jules "in his soiled artist's coat, his tie on backward, his shirt flung off and draped across three chairs, stamping his foot or breaking the fire tongs in the heat of our discussions."

Jules and she—or "my pseudonym and I," as Aurore used to refer to them—gave much to each other psychologically. Jules was highly sensitive, subject to black depressions and a victim of lazy habits. Aurore helped him tolerate human society and encouraged him to work. For her part, Aurore "needed a soul which burned to love me as I knew how to love and to console me for all the miseries of my childhood and my youth."

"Though I am already old," she wrote in a letter to an intimate friend a few months before her twenty-seventh birthday, "I have found a heart as young as mine. When I was weary of existence and only put up with it because of my children, Jules brought me back to life. When I had nothing but revulsion for the future, he turned it into a beautiful vista. Now it is filled with him and his sweet, frank nature, filled with his work, his hopes. . . ." But not all of Aurore's Berrichon friends agreed with her about Sandeau's nature. Some found him too glum, others saw him as too ambitious and plagued with petty vanities. Aurore was not blind to their feelings, yet she was constantly excusing his frailties, constantly urging mutual friends to be kind and good to Jules.

As March drew to a close, Aurore realized that soon her three months in Paris would be over. She contemplated her imminent departure with a divided heart. One half of it lay with her children, whom she longed to rejoin. But the other half lay with Jules, with her friends, with the stimulating intellectual life of the capital she hated to leave. She was determined, however, to hold to her agreement with Casimir and, the first week in April, she reserved herself a seat in a stagecoach.

Though news of her journalistic career had leaked out to the family by now, and she had written Casimir about her first achievements as a breadwinner, she was greeted in Nohant by her husband and Hippolyte as if she had done no more than return from a brief holiday. Neither one was about to admit to being wrong. She found them more or less as she had left them . . . her brother "a bit ill from drinking too much," her husband "shouting loudly and eating well." During her absence, her children's tutor had kept her faithfully informed by letter about their health and progress, and she was overjoyed at the sight of them. She had been afraid they would forget her, but she was hugged tightly by little Solange, a rambunctious child "as beautiful as an angel." Seven-year-old Maurice proudly showed off the National Guard uniform with red-plumed headdress his mother had sent to him from Paris. He was "in raptures" at the sight of her and "almost smothered me with his kisses."

Aurore spent part of her days teaching her son Latin and helping her daughter with her first halting French lessons. Later she would retire to her study to write. Beyond the window, spring winds were chasing storm clouds, the first rosebushes were in bloom, and there was a fresh greenness everywhere. When she glanced up from her page momentarily, her eyes fell on the pressed plants she had collected over the years or some rare stone or pretty shell arranged on the shelves over her desk. From her mother, the daughter of a bird keeper, Aurore had inherited an unusual gift for taming birds. Sometimes a shy warbler, which would instantly flee at the approach of anyone else, would fly right into Aurore's study to settle on her shoulder or to eat a crumb from her hand. She trained her bird friends to sit quietly while she wrote, and she set to work on a short piece inspired by her visit to the cathedral of Saint Étienne at Bourges. In addition she began a political melodrama "black as fifty devils, with plotters, executioners, assassins, daggers, blood and dark curses."

But though they absorbed and excited her, Aurore did not bother to discuss her writings with Casimir. The gulf between them had grown wider than ever and each had abandoned hope of bridging it. "My husband does exactly as he pleases," Aurore wrote her mother. "Whether he has mistresses or doesn't have them, whether he drinks wine or water, saves money or spends it, builds, plants, alters, buys, manages his wealth and his house as he sees fit—all that is no concern of mine. It is only fair, however, that I should have the same liberty. If my husband were to refuse me that, he would become contemptible in my eyes and that is something he doesn't wish. I am entirely independent therefore. I go to bed when he gets up, I can go to La Châtre or even to Rome, I can come home at midnight or at six in the morning—it's my business and no one else's. Those who find it wrong and who make ugly remarks to you about me must simply be judged by your good sense and a mother's heart."

All the same Aurore felt the "interminable solitude"

at Nohant and began to count the days before her departure. It was only her children now who held her there, and in the future she would come home—at irregular intervals but conscientiously—just to be with Maurice and Solange. Even as she left them again in July, she thought to herself, "If it weren't for the hope I have of being more useful to them one day with the pen of a scribe than with a housewife's thread and needle, I would not leave."

But there was another compelling reason, too, for her to hurry off to Paris. She had already ceased to think of writing merely as a means of earning her living. In a letter to a friend, she affirmed, "I am more than ever determined to follow a literary career. Despite the distasteful sides of it which I encounter at times, despite days of laziness or fatigue which come to interrupt my work, despite the more than modest way I have learned to live, I feel that my life from now on will always be full. I have a purpose, a task, let me say it right out, *a passion*. The calling of a writer is violent and well-nigh indestructible—once it gets hold of you, it never lets go."

Back in Paris, Aurore not only continued to write articles for the press, she suggested to Jules that they collaborate on a novel. Her first efforts in this medium she had long since laid aside, for she had come to agree with Latouche that they were "abominable." Now, however, she felt that she and her "pseudonym" had enough experience to produce a popular and saleable work. Jules agreed. They invented a story, set in the Pyrenees mountains, about a nun and an actress, and they approached a publisher and secured a cash advance. Soon they started writing the first chapters of a novel they called *Rose et Blanche.*

Aurore no longer lived on the rue de Seine but in an apartment on the quai Saint-Michel, a sixth-floor haven where sparrows nested in the greenery on the balcony and a wide view stretched beyond the wrought-iron railing toward the river Seine and the towers of Notre-Dame cathedral. Jules and Aurore lived together and shared a frugal existence. There was no staff of servants as at Nohant, only a cleaning woman who came in from time to time. Aurore either flung their meals together or ordered them from a café down the street, while she washed and ironed the laundry herself. At that, she was not always able to stay within the limits of her budget, but she still managed somehow to entertain modestly the growing number of friends she and Jules had begun to attract.

Among these new friends was Honoré de Balzac, a writer whose genius was just beginning to be recognized. Balzac was a stout but powerful man in his early thirties, overflowing with intellectual energy and high spirits. Like Aurore, he had in his childhood been deprived of a mother's love; he had been shipped out to live with strangers. Unlike her, however, he had been forced to make his living at an early age. His attempts at establishing a printing house of his own had ended in a financial disaster which set a pattern for his life— he always found himself writing under pressure to pay his bills. He was so exacting in his artistic demands upon himself that the numerous corrections with which he blackened proof sheets, which had to be printed all over again at great cost, often placed him heavily in debt before a book appeared. But some of his bills accumulated simply because he loved to surround himself with beautiful furniture and works of art, and to eat the finest of foods.

Balzac grew fond of Jules and Aurore and often came to visit them, "climbing up, with his great stomach, all the flights of our building at quai Saint-Michel," Aurore recalled later. "He would arrive puffing and laughing and immediately start talking before he had caught his breath. Sometimes he used to pick up the papers strewn over my worktable, throw a brief glance at them as if to see what they were all about, but then suddenly he would think of some book of his own he was in the process of writing and begin to tell us its story. He would often tell it in an impossible way, full of fire and spirit but with neither order nor clarity. It was a kind of mad flight of words, for he threw away only the overflow of his thoughts and kept their profound wisdom for his works."

Aurore found him, as posterity would, "an unequaled master in painting modern society and the human race." She felt that she learned a great deal from the long hours she spent listening to Balzac and exchanging ideas with him on literature.

"You are seeking to describe man as he ought to be," he said to her once, "while I take him as he is. Believe me, we are both right. The two paths lead to the same destination. As you do, I like exceptional beings. I am one myself. But crude common creatures interest me more than they do you. I make them larger than life, I idealize them in reverse by revealing their ugliness or stupidity, while you do not wish to look at people or at things which give you nightmares."

Aurore argued that books which lent hope to readers, who lived harsh and bitter existences in a materialistic society, had certainly as much value as those which showed only the base and seamy aspects of life. She even refused to listen one day when Balzac tried to read her some of the spicier passages from his *Droll Stories.* Fairly throwing the book in his face, she called him "fat and indecent." Storming out the room, he roared back, "Stupid prude!"

But Aurore and Balzac were only better friends for such altercations, for fundamentally both had generous natures. Often she and Jules would go to Balzac's apartment on the rue Cassini, where the walls were hung with lace-bordered silk and where Balzac, who would rather deprive himself of soup than of silverware, lived in want in the midst of superfluity. There was only one room left bare and unfurnished, a monklike study in which the author would sit writing for twelve to sixteen hours at a stretch.

One night after having dined there on boiled beef, melon and champagne frappé, Jules and Aurore saw Balzac put on a new elegant dressing gown, which he showed off to them proudly. Then, taking up a candle, he offered to conduct them in this attire as far as the gates of the Luxembourg Gardens. It was late, the area was deserted, and Aurore remarked that he might well be assassinated on his way back home.

"Not at all," rejoined Balzac. "If I meet thieves, they will either take me for a madman and be frightened away, or they will take me for a prince and withdraw respectfully."

"It was a beautiful calm night," she recalled. "He

Honoré de Balzac. Photograph by Nadar.

accompanied us, carrying his lighted candle in a lovely ornate gilt holder, and talking to us about four Arabian horses which he did not have yet but which he would soon possess and which he never came to own though he always firmly believed they would be his. He would have walked us all the way to the other end of Paris if we had let him.''

In December of 1831, the novel Aurore and Jules had written was published. The critics received *Rose et Blanche* favorably and it was a commercial success. Only Jules had signed his name to it—abbreviating Jules Sandeau to J. Sand—and Aurore's participation was not publicly known. Yet she had done at least an equal share of the work and she had every reason to feel encouraged about her future as a writer.

Strangely enough, she was not. At this time she was strongly influenced by her editor at the *Figaro*, Latouche, even more than by Balzac. Hypercritical, Latouche was given to meticulous dissection of those around him, which often reduced them to nonentities. Over the past months he had so bludgeoned Aurore with his advice that "I was cramped by his rigid dicta. I was learning everything a writer should not do, nothing that he ought to do, and was losing all confidence in myself." As a final blow—when *Rose et Blanche* appeared—Latouche summarily condemned it.

"You know nothing of the world or the people in it," he said to Aurore. "You simply take over other people's thoughts. Your own brain is a hollow shell." Her work was a *pastiche*, he added, an "imitation" of the Romantics. And in her memoirs she later admitted, "I told myself that he was right. I returned to Nohant, my mind made up to go back to decorating tea boxes and cigar cases."

Once back at Nohant, however, she sat down at her writing desk. "Without hope, without any idea where I was going with it," she began another novel. It became the story of a young woman who is trapped in a loveless marriage. The heroine, whose name is Indiana, is a passionate Creole awakened to real love for the first time by the adoration of a young man. She is ready to be cast out by the strict and conservative society in which she lives in order to live with him, when he chooses instead a marriage of convenience with a rich woman. In the end a cousin of hers, himself a victim in the past of an arranged marriage though all his life he has secretly loved Indiana, rescues her from a severe illness after her husband's sudden death. She falls in love with him and they go off to a thatched cottage on an island to live the kind of free and happy love idyll they could not possibly live within society. "Go back to society" a sympathetic stranger is told in the last lines of the book. "But if ever it banishes you, think of us and our Indian thatched hut."

With nothing but a glass of milk or lemonade at her side—and a bowl of water in which she extinguished the cigarettes she smoked—Aurore worked every night for six weeks from seven in the evening until dawn to complete her book. She called it *Indiana*, and she gave it a preface in which she spoke directly to the reader:

"I bring to you a sad tableau of social miseries and show you needs, desires, human passions imprisoned by the laws of our world." A story which mingled romance with social comment, it was above all an exposure of the "injustice of the barbarian laws which govern the existence of women in marriage, in the family and in society."

The writing was not designed to fit the demands of any particular fashion or literary school—she had thrown aside all such demands when she began it. Nor had she given any special thought to whether anyone would want to read her outpourings. She had simply put her own experience in marriage and the convictions born of that experience into a book, and she had no idea what its fate would be. She placed it in her trunk, however, and gathering up three-year-old Solange to take with her this time, she went to Paris to find out.

5

Jules Sandeau, who was the first to read *Indiana*, was overcome with astonishment. It was a bit too serious for his taste, yet the writing was finer than anything he felt he himself could have done. For all his admiration for it, however, he refused to lend his name to a work to which he had not contributed a solitary word. Aurore was thus presented with a dilemma. She could not use her own name, for her husband's family had made it clear from the start that they did not wish to see Dudevant "printed on the covers of a book." At the same time *Rose et Blanche* had sold so well that the publisher had demanded another novel from the pen of "J. Sand"—the pseudonym she and Jules Sandeau had employed—and he wanted no other name now on *In-*

diana. Aurore took her dilemma to the editor of the *Figaro.* Latouche made the suggestion that she retain "Sand" but invent a new first name for herself. She thought quickly and produced "George." In ancient Greek, George stood for "a man of the earth," and it seemed to her a good choice for someone who came from the peasant countryside of Berry. Her solution satisfied both Jules and the publisher, and *Indiana* went to the printers over the signature "G. Sand."

While waiting for her novel to appear, Aurore went back to her writing desk in her apartment on the quai Saint-Michel, though she and Jules began to alter their life there now for the sake of the new member of the household—Solange. There were no more late nights at the theater, no more irregular hours. They ate their meals at home and went for walks along the grass-bordered paths of the Jardin des Plantes, adjusting their pace to the short strides of the little girl.

Solange was a willful creature. Sometimes she would slyly throw her shoes into the bushes when no one was looking so that her mother would be forced to carry her home from the garden and up five flights. But there was usually something comical and winning about her pranks that made it impossible for Aurore to scold her, and Jules grew fond of the child. He observed her with amusement as she tried to tape back together the flower stems she had broken in her mother's hanging garden on the balcony, and he enjoyed watching her being tucked in on the sofa where she slept. So it was not this quiet domestic existence which made Jules begin to feel the first glimmerings of resentment.

Writing came hard to the indolent Jules, while it appeared to come effortlessly to Aurore. He would try to work, but sit motionless while, at his elbow, page after completed page would fly out from under her pen. Aurore's unflagging industry irritated him, his suspicion that she was more gifted than he humiliated him, and before long he began to quarrel with her. When she urged him to write, Jules insisted that he had every intention of writing but that unfortunately he had not been born, as obviously she had, with "a little steel spring" in his brain—he was incapable of just pressing a button and setting his imagination going!

Jules' dwindling self-respect led him to other women, and when Aurore found out, she felt as shocked and hurt by his infidelity as she had been by Casimir's. Her morality firmly rejected promiscuity. It was not until many months later, however, that she could bring herself to face the final rupture which occurred between them, when she sent Jules away for good. In the meantime, *Indiana* had made its appearance.

When Aurore received her first copy of the book, she sat down to write a dedication in it to Latouche. As she was writing it, Latouche himself appeared at her apartment and, seizing the volume, began to leaf through it —curious, uneasy, in an especially bristling mood that day. Aurore withdrew to the balcony and waited for his verdict. It came in the form of a word she had heard before.

"Pastiche!" he exclaimed. "Imitation . . . School of Balzac! What do you want me to say . . . ?"

Book in hand, he pursued her onto the balcony and began to point out to her, in passage after passage, how she had tried to ape the great writer but had succeeded

91

only in being neither Balzac nor herself. Fuming, he left the apartment. The next day she awoke to find a note from him.

"George, I offer you my deepest apologies," he wrote. "Forget my harshness yesterday, forget all the hard words I have spoken to you over the last six months. No woman alive today can be compared to you. I spent the night reading your book. My child, I am proud of you. . . ."

George—for that is how she began to think of herself now and what all her close friends began to call her too —was relieved and pleased. Despite Latouche's words, however, the most she modestly hoped for *Indiana* was that it should "pass unnoticed in the crowd of bad or mediocre new books" which flooded the market every year. Instead she discovered that such distinguished men of letters as the critic Sainte-Beuve, the redoubtable reviewer Gustave Planche, whose cruel pen terrorized authors, and Honoré de Balzac, along with half a score of others writing in the major journals of Paris, greeted it favorably. As George Sand later recalled in her autobiography, "The newspapers all spoke of Mr. G. Sand in terms of the highest praise. They insinuated that the hand of a woman must have slipped in here and there to reveal to the author certain subtleties of the heart and the mind, though they declared that the style and the perceptions had such power that they could only have been the work of a man."

George discovered that she was no longer a suppliant at publishers' doors. *Indiana* quickly went into several new printings and was adapted for the stage, with two separate theatrical productions of it playing in Paris in the year that followed its publication. The book's commercial success made George's dream of economic independence from her husband realizable. She was more than ready to fulfill the requests which came flooding in. Her publishers negotiated a contract for *Valentine*, a novel she was already writing. She finished the book and it appeared, six months later, advertised as a work from the pen of "G. Sand, author of *Indiana*." The *Revue de Paris* needed stories and she wrote two for them. The editor François Buloz, who had a rare gift for discovering new talent, was attracting to the pages of his *Revue des Deux Mondes* the finest writers, poets, historians, philosophers and journalists of the nineteenth century. He sent an offer to George and soon she signed to write for his review under an arrangement by which she could earn as much as four thousand francs a year.

Latouche, who had retired from the *Figaro* to live in the country, gave over his "blue attic" on the quai Malaquais to George. It was a sunny apartment on the fourth floor, beneath the eaves, with a living room papered in blue. It overlooked a tree-filled garden where a small fountain played. In one of the bedrooms George set up Solange's iron-posted bed, while in the blue living room, with its cozy fireplace, she found room for her piano. Almost every day the stairway was crowded with admiring strangers who came to meet the celebrated author. The world at large still believed "G. Sand" to be a man, and visitors to the quai Malaquais were astonished when they were received by a modest, slender, attractive woman.

The followers of Saint-Simon—opponents of the

Establishment, who were struggling against social inequality and the barriers of class—rejoiced at the appearance of *Indiana* and of *Valentine* as well. This second novel portrayed a hopeless romance between a woman of the aristocracy and the son of a poor farmer, a democratic theme unusual in those days. The Saint-Simonists felt they had discovered in Sand a new champion.

George was thoroughly disconcerted. She had tried "faithfully to portray man as he is," but she had not consciously sought to be the champion of any particular cause or creed. She was not equipped at all for such a role, she felt. Ever since her unhappy childhood she had hated what she considered the unfair privileges of the wealthy classes. Recently, with sympathetic pain, she had seen that hatred mirrored in the eyes of Parisian working people whose tenements had been ravaged by a cholera epidemic and whose existences had been rendered intolerable by poverty and unemployment. From her window at quai Saint-Michel, she had watched them raise their clenched fists to the sky in impotent rebellion. With Solange in her arms, she had been caught in a riot when Parisian workers demonstrated in the streets, only to be hunted down later and shot by government troops. But at the same time "there was nothing in my old beliefs which was strong enough to help me struggle against the rule of monied interests in society, and I was unable to find in the new republican and socialist ideas enough light to combat the shade with which Mammon had covered the world." She shied away from taking an active part in politics and hastened back to the quiet refuge of her study.

In the same way she tried to retreat from the limelight that the popularity of her two novels had thrust upon her. She hated publicity but was forced to hide her distaste for it when she saw that most people merely took her attitude for an affectation. Her achievements, though they naturally brought her satisfaction, troubled her in another way. "The success of *Indiana* frightens me considerably," she admitted in a letter to a friend. "Before, I had always thought of working quietly, on inconsequential things, without attracting too much attention. Fate, it seems, has decided otherwise. Now I feel I must justify the undeserved praise I have received. It is upsetting to a person of my nature."

Quite apart from the difficulty of adjusting to unexpected success, the rift with Jules Sandeau had left her bewildered and unhappy. She had thought that once the enslaving restrictions of marriage were removed, love would thrive and endure. She had discovered painfully that this was not always the case. In her loneliness and disappointment she had no thought of returning to her husband; on her side the break had been final, while he wished to know as little as possible of his wife's career or her personal life when she was absent in Paris. She brought her despair to her writing desk and began a new novel, which she eventually called *Lélia.*

In this novel she examined the various solaces offered by the world—religion, carnal passion, cold skepticism, naive idealism, stoicism—making each of her characters the embodiment of an idea. Less a story than a philosophical prose poem, it was not anything she expected to publish. She was simply writing it as a "sort of sad release into reverie, a way of insulating myself from reality, of synthesizing my own doubts and suffering." In her novel, she found every solution inadequate except perhaps stoicism, where reason and self-command conquer the unsatisfied desires of the heart. In her real life, however, she could not achieve any such victory. "Alas, how brief are my hours of common sense and strength!" she wrote a friend. "How stingy God has been to me with his consolations! How weary I am of being devoured by this constant thirst for the *unrealizable*." While she labored at *Lélia* off and on, picking it up and dropping it time and again, she continued to write and publish articles and short stories.

For all that George tried to avoid curiosity seekers and closed her ears when she heard people at concerts or at the theater pointing her out in loud whispers to their neighbors, she welcomed the acquaintance of leading figures in literature and art. One of these was Charles Augustin Sainte-Beuve. Though he was no older than George, his writings had already gained him a formidable reputation as a critic and poet. He was a plump young man with quick, darting eyes. At once shrewd and impressionable, spiteful and affectionate, Sainte-Beuve was never able to straighten out his own personal life. He was unhappily in love with a woman who did not belong to him—the wife of Victor Hugo. All the same he took a special pleasure in interfering in other people's lives, giving them advice in both literary and sentimental matters. George needed such a friend and soon Sainte-Beuve became her informal confessor. She grew accustomed to showing him her unfinished writings, for she appreciated his keen, critical eye, and later in life, she counted him among her "intellectual educators and benefactors."

A friend of Sainte-Beuve's also became George's friend—the Romantic writer Prosper Mérimée, author of plays and stories including the short novel *Carmen*, upon which Georges Bizet based his opera. In his disdain for conservative tradition, Mérimée's Romantic rebellion took the form of a cynical, disabused outlook on life. Personally, he had the reputation of a Don Juan, and when his roving eye settled on the slim, dark-haired woman who had stolen her way into the literary profession, he set out to capture her heart.

In the beginning, George avoided Mérimée, ignoring his pressing notes to her or at the last minute canceling appointments he had made with her. Still, she was fascinated by his powerful intellect, by a calm strength she found in him, and gradually he overcame her reluctance. Soon Paris society was amused by the sight of the twenty-nine-year-old libertine bearing the sleeping Solange on his shoulders as he stood at the top of the grand staircase at the Opéra with George Sand. It seemed for a moment that George had domesticated Mérimée, but actually their brief relationship was unsatisfactory on both sides. George found that her feelings froze up inside her under Mérimée's cool, jaded gaze. Mérimée himself was abashed to discover that his virility abandoned him in the presence of this often shy yet formidable woman. Though they remained casual friends afterward, neither one much regretted the end of their intimacy, which had engaged the idle gossips of the capital for a few short weeks.

More wounded than ever by her unsatisfactory relationships with men, George began to wonder if there was something missing in her own makeup . . . a worry which increased when she met the actress Marie Dorval. A dazzling and gifted woman, Dorval was at the height of her career, playing leading roles in dramas by Victor Hugo and Alexandre Dumas. Though she worked every night behind the footlights, the idol of Paris audiences found time after her performances to drop in at the quai Malaquais for long talks. George was fascinated by the uninhibited Dorval, who spoke with candor of her love affairs in the past and of her passion at the moment for the poet Alfred de Vigny. And George was filled with admiration for the abandon with which this extroverted woman gave vent to her feelings. In comparison she felt herself to be "cold, incomplete, paralyzed."

With Dorval's image in mind, George began to expand the original draft of her novel *Lélia* to include two contrasting female types. One was a courtesan whose untamed spirit in many ways mirrored Dorval's. The character of Lélia, on the other hand, longed for love yet had been so hurt by love that she had become repressed, afraid, incapable of consummating her desires. In many ways she was a portrait of George's despairing view of herself.

Lélia was much more than a book about women and about love, however. It was an exposure of the religious doubts which were assailing many people in France at that time. The book offered no answers, for George herself knew no answers which would lift her out of her despair. Still, her probings had a telling effect, it appeared. One evening when Sainte-Beuve came to dine at the quai Malaquais, George read him her partly finished manuscript, and the next day she received a letter from the critic.

"You are a woman, you are under thirty," Sainte-Beuve wrote, "and yet you have a mind which has sounded the very depths of human experience without its leaving the slightest outward trace upon you. You are able to carry within you knowledge which would seam men's brows, turn men's hair white, and write of it in a calm, controlled way, with ease and lightness. All of this I admire in the extreme. You possess, Madame, a rare and powerful nature." *Lélia*, with its philosophical cast, was not the sort of book which would appeal to the general public, he told her, yet he found it an exceptional work and he urged her to go on with it.

George was well into the second volume by now; she had decided she would publish it after all and soon hoped to see *Lélia* in print. In the meantime, though she gratefully accepted Sainte-Beuve's appraisal of her work, she was less willing to accept his attempts to introduce her to the men he knew. When he wrote her that he would like her to meet a philosopher friend, George agreed but then, losing courage, backed out. She had no desire to repeat her experience with Mérimée or, in fact, to become involved with any man at all.

Sainte-Beuve, however, persisted. He knew, as he wrote, that "in her first encounters" George was "embarrassed, silent, unable in the least to give the impression she would have liked to give." Later, when she grew more at ease, people were drawn to her warmth and her receptivity, for she was above all a good listener. He suggested now that he bring the poet Alfred de Musset around to see her.

99

Musset had made a dazzling debut with poetic works in which the romantic idealism of a dreamer warred with the shattered illusions of a debauchee. Handsome as the English poet Lord Byron, whom he emulated in dress and manners, he was weary of the world and of women at twenty-two. George admitted she was curious to meet this young genius and at first agreed to meet him; but then in a few days she wrote to Sainte-Beuve, "By the way, I've been thinking about it, and I don't want you to bring Alfred de Musset. He is very much a dandy, and I am sure we would not get on together."

But she was unable to avoid Alfred de Musset. François Buloz, the editor of the *Revue des Deux Mondes*, was in the habit of giving dinner parties for his writers. At one of them George found herself placed beside a young man wearing a velvet collar that reached to his slim waist, and sky blue, tight-fitting trousers; he bore an air of casual and exotic elegance. Alfred de Musset shone that evening. He was witty, gracious, thoroughly agreeable. To her surprise, George found that he was neither "light-minded nor dissolute, though he would like to have appeared to be both."

Musset in turn was intrigued by the woman at his side who wore a little decorative dagger dangling from her belt, and who was silent except when she laughed at his witticisms. Later he recalled her appearance . . . "dark-haired, pale, her olive skin touched with bronze highlights and great eyes, like an Indian's." One evening soon afterward, he picked up a copy of her first novel and began to read it, occasionally drawing his pen through a superfluous adjective. When he finished, he composed a short poem.

The next day, George found a brief, formal, properly flattering letter from him, the sort a colleague of short acquaintance would write another in praise of his work. It was signed with the traditional phrase, "Believe me, Madame, yours most respectfully . . ." But in the poem, entitled "After Reading *Indiana*," Musset spoke to her intimately and the questions he posed were deeply personal. Referring to a love scene in the novel, he asked, in his verses, whether someone else had dictated "that burning page" to her or she herself had lived it. And when love "seeks in vain the ghost of a lost illusion," he asked again, ". . . Has thine own heart known that sadness?" And then again, when she wrote of "ecstasies without happiness full of an immense void," he probed, "Didst thou dream that, George, or was it a memory?"

The same day, she responded to Musset's letter. Adroitly avoiding his questions, she thanked him for his praise of her work, praised his still more, and sent him an invitation: "When I had the honor of meeting you, I did not dare ask you to my place. I am still afraid that its austerity will frighten you off or bore you. However, if some afternoon you should feel tired of worldly pleasures and tempted to enter the cell of a recluse, you would be received with gratitude and cordiality."

Musset accepted, and before long the two authors became friends. He continued to sign his letters formally, while she signed hers simply "George Sand"; but they talked freely and easily when they were together, discussing art, politics, literature. . . . When *Lélia* was about to appear, in July of 1833, George sent Musset a set of proofs. He wrote her that "feeling joy in reading something beautifully done is the privilege of old

Alfred de Musset. Portrait by Charles Landelle.

friendship. I have no such rights over you, Madame, nevertheless I must tell you how *Lélia* impresses me. In it there are scores of pages which go straight to the heart, frankly, vigorously, and which are as beautiful as anything in *René* and in *Lara.*" (These works of Chateaubriand and of Byron were idolized by the Romantic writers.) "If it weren't for *Lélia*," Musset added, "you would have been just Madame So-and-So who wrote books. Now you are George Sand."

Musset's growing admiration for George seemed to make him feel a need to define the nature of their relations. "You know me well enough by now," he wrote her in the same letter, "to realize that you will never hear from my lips the ridiculous words *Will you? Or won't you?* In such matters there lies between us a Baltic Sea. You can only offer a man a moral love—and I can give that to no one. But I can be . . . not your friend—even that has too moral a ring to it for me—but a kind of inconsequential comrade, without rights and thus neither jealous nor quarrelsome . . . simply someone who will come and smoke up your tobacco, muss up your belongings and catch head colds philosophizing with you under all the chestnut trees of modern Europe."

Such a definition suited George to perfection. She was not in love with Musset. And she had less desire than ever now to be swept up by the storms of a new passion, for she had another sort of storm on her hands. The publication of *Lélia* had been greeted by a sharply divided press. Each side was engaged in a battle of words with its adversary and George's reputation was caught in the cross fire.

Its supporters eulogized the book, which dealt

frankly and penetratingly with women, love, religion. One critic praised the "incredible magnificence of its style." Another remarked that "among the voices calling for a more equitable part for women in intellectual life and in the expression of serious ideas," George Sand was "by far the most courageous and the most eloquent." The opponents of the novel, on the other hand, attacked it fiercely. One reviewer declared it to be "a dangerous book . . . revolting to the human nature which it pretends to enlighten, bringing disorder and ruin to our social edifice." Another commented on what he considered its "licentiousness and cynicism," while still another found in its "corrosive pages ignoble and shameful thoughts."

While the scandal surrounding the book caused its already mounting sales to soar, the battle in the press intensified. Gustave Planche, who had praised it in the *Revue des Deux Mondes*, wrote to the critic who had condemned it in *L'Europe littéraire* and challenged him to a duel. The feuding critics named their seconds, and one morning in a clearing among the trees in the Bois de Boulogne, they drew their pistols. Both were poor shots and no one was wounded, but the event added to *Lélia*'s notoriety.

George fought the attacks against her in her own way. She wrote letters of rebuke to her silent supporters among the critics who had not come to her defense. As for "ugly insults" directed at her personally by those who raged against her "perverted mind, odious character, obscene pen," she brushed them aside. "I often get mud on my shoes when I walk in the streets," she wrote, "but I wipe it off before I enter my friends' homes.

There is mud in such statements and I have to take it, but I don't have to keep it on me."

Many readers identified George, whom by now they knew to be a woman, with her fictional heroine. Some of her friends, embarrassed at associating with the "abominable Lélia" the critics had condemned, began avoiding her, but Musset was not among them. Young though he was, he was an old warrior who had received his own wounds more than once at the hands of the press. Her "inconsequential comrade" merely increased his visits. But as he saw more and more of George, he found himself in a predicament which surprised him and which he at last felt forced to explain.

"My dear George," he wrote her, "I have something stupid and ridiculous to tell you. I am in love with you. I've been in love with you since the first day I came to see you. I thought that I could cure myself by keeping our relations merely on a friendly basis. There are many things in your character which would contribute to such a cure, and I have tried to convince myself of it. But the moments I spend with you are costing me too much. I don't expect to gain anything from you by telling you this. I will simply lose a friend and the only agreeable hours I have known this whole past month. George, I am mad to deprive myself of the pleasure of seeing you . . . but the truth is that I'm suffering and I haven't the strength to keep silent."

George hesitated to respond to the plea in Musset's letter. She took love seriously, yet wondered if the erratic genius, the dissolute youth in Musset, would take it so too. She could not know. She was not even sure she loved him. And while she hesitated, Musset continued to write—more ardently, more despairingly—to "a human being who is capable of understanding me." At times he was hopeful and pleaded with her: "If my name is written in a corner of your heart, no matter how faint the imprint or faded the ink, do not rub it out." At other times he abandoned hope. "Love those who know how to love, I know only how to suffer. Farewell, George . . ."

At last he received a note asking him to come at midnight. He arrived at the appointed hour at the blue attic on the quai Malaquais and did not leave in the next hours nor even in the days that followed. At the end of a month George wrote Sainte-Beuve: "A man's love combined with the friendship of a comrade is something I did not know existed. I never expected to discover it anywhere, least of all where I have found it." Musset himself was surprised at his liaison with an intellectual woman. Before he had met George, he had known only "ecstacies without happiness" in the perfumed boudoirs of bejeweled courtesans . . . "larvas without heads," he called them, "without hearts, without souls—in a word, slaves." Now he was discovering that "supreme joy lay in embracing with heart and mind another heart, another mind."

Beyond his adoration, too, was the poet's profound gratitude. He felt that George was rescuing his genius from the slow suicide of his dissipated life. Of course, she had the disconcerting habit of rising in the middle of the night to go to work at her desk to meet a deadline. But this amused Musset rather than irritated him. When he was not working himself, he wrote jingles about her as she sat "between two potted plants puffing upon her cigarette" and filling pages with her rapid hand. Or, gifted artist that he was, he sketched her. When people came to dinner, he enjoyed playing practical jokes which he knew would make George laugh. One night he disguised himself as a serving maid and, in a short dress with a cross dangling at his throat, he waited on the table in a deliberately bungling and clumsy way, spilling a pitcher of water on the head of a distinguished philosopher.

George rejoiced at the youthful gaiety Musset brought to the quai Malaquais, which totally transformed the atmosphere—and transformed her too. She and Musset were the talk of literary Paris and, though some considered them an oddly matched couple, no one could deny that George's face had lost its melancholy cast. Resplendent in her happiness, she looked ten years younger.

In early August, George and Musset decided to take a holiday together. They journeyed to Fontainebleau, where they explored the vast, dark forests. Sometimes George would stride on ahead like a soldier, singing at the top of her lungs. At other times, their arms entwined, their voices a murmur, they meandered along the sandy paths among the flowering heather and the savage rocks. Years later, in one of his most famous poems, "Souvenir," Musset recalled the days he spent with George in the deserted beauty of the forest "where all my youth, like a flock of birds, sings to the sound of my footsteps."

But for George, the holiday was marred by a bizarre incident. One moonlight night in the woods, Musset suffered a hallucination. He believed he saw a darting ghost—pale, its clothing rent, its hair flying. The wasted features were those of a debauched man twenty years older than he, with wild eyes and a brutally twisted mouth. Stricken with fear, the poet flung himself to the ground, convinced that the specter he had seen was himself. His fit of delirium lasted a quarter of an hour. When it passed, Musset became harsh and irascible, willfully choosing the direction opposite any George suggested, so that they were forced to spend the entire night trudging exhaustedly through the forest before they reached their hotel. The next day, Musset had totally recovered. He was pleasant and agreeable. He even joked about the incident, drawing a comic caricature of himself and of George in her tattered clothing. But it was the first time she had witnessed one of the poet's spells, which came over him occasionally when he drank or when his nerves were strained, and she was unable to laugh.

Back in Paris, George shook off the troubling impression the incident made upon her, and soon she and Musset were planning a new voyage, this time to Italy. To pay her way, George reached an agreement with Buloz, who gave her money for two stories which would appear in the *Revue des Deux Mondes*, as well as an advance on a novel which she promised to complete during her travels. In those days, a woman had to gain her husband's permission before the authorities would grant her a passport to leave the country. George had been plagued off and on by rheumatism since her years spent in the dank convent cell, and when she wrote Casimir now that she wished to travel for a few months to a warmer climate, he raised no objections.

She arranged for the care of her children during her absence. She persuaded friends in Paris to take Maurice out on the days he was free from his boarding school, and she sent Solange back to her father in Nohant. Musset, short of funds as even successful poets often were, obtained money from his family to pay his own expenses. And in mid-December of 1833, George and Musset mounted a coach heading southward along the road to Italy.

6

The journey to Genoa was long and arduous, especially because it was winter, but George combined the hardiness of a Berrichon countrywoman with a provincial's curiosity about unknown places. Gazing at the passing landscape and quite at ease in a pair of pearl gray trousers and man's cap, she ignored the discomforts of the drafty, lurching stagecoach. The hypersensitive Musset, however, was jarred painfully by every rut in the road and could only hold his aching head in his hands.

On the boat down the Rhône river, they discovered among their fellow passengers Henri Beyle, a relatively unknown novelist whose works had enjoyed little success. Under the pseudonym of Stendhal, he had written *The Red and the Black* and would later write *The Charterhouse of Parma*, both of which would become classics of world literature. Heedless of the fierce cold and of the poor food they had just eaten in a mediocre inn, George gave herself over to the pleasure of talking with

Stendhal, whom she considered "one of the most re-markable writers of our time." For Musset, however, a holiday consisted of wandering through museums and churches, wining and dining on exotic food in the finest restaurants, and passing luxurious days in a warm bed. He could not wait to reach Italy. In Avignon they parted from Stendhal to travel on to Marseilles, where they boarded a ship and set out across the Mediterranean. While George calmly smoked a cigar on deck, her feet set wide apart to balance herself on the rolling vessel, Musset spent most of the crossing running from cabin to rail in an agony of seasickness.

The sight of the rain-drenched Italian port city of Genoa where they landed did not raise the poet's spir-its. He noted that George, though herself sick now with a severe cold, was eager to get down to work. Financial necessity forced her to put in at least five hours a day at her writing desk, but Musset began to rankle. An artist was not a slave, he insisted, and when she locked her door to him in order to work undisturbed, he called her "a nun, a bore." Soon he took to leaving her in the hotel room while he went out to explore the dives and brothels of Genoa. He would return late at night, not only drunk but proudly recounting his exploits. There was something gratuitously cruel in this which revealed the poet's dual nature.

"I have never seen more frightening contrasts em-bodied in a single individual," George wrote of him later. "There are two people in him. One of them is all goodness, sweetness, tenderness, openness and inno-cence. The other is violent, despotic, suspicious, hard and as petty and selfish as possible. The latter exults in evil as much as the other man in him exults in good."

Musset was aware of these warring elements in himself. They were born, in part, of the disenchantment he shared with an entire generation of young Romantics. He, like others, had been reared on the democratic ideals of the French Revolution, only to feel, a few short decades later, that those ideals had been trampled underfoot by a hypocritical, money-minded society. When asked in what it believed, "the youth of France," he wrote, "raising its wine glass with a hand that was thirsting to hold a sword instead, answered: *In nothing.*" And yet some part of Musset believed still, if faintly, in a future where "there will not be one stalk of grain higher than any other in the human harvest," and he dreamed of an era of "free men." Meantime, caught between "that which is no longer and that which has not yet come into being," he often found himself wandering in despair in that mental no-man's-land which he labeled *la maladie du siècle*, the "sickness of the century."

George understood this about the poet. She was by now deeply in love with him. Overlooking what she considered his temporary lapses in Genoa, she traveled on with him to Livorno, Pisa, Florence, Ferrara. . . . In Venice, with its marble palaces, medieval houses and carved bridges built on islands divided by waterways where colorful gondolas drifted by, they settled into the Hotel Danieli. But in this setting, unsurpassed for its romantic beauty, Musset informed George regretfully that he was no longer in love with her. They tried hard to reestablish the old comradely relationship they had once enjoyed, but it was hopeless. Musset soon took to haunting the slums of Venice, staying out half the night

George Sand before a stone balustrade in Venice. Drawing by Alfred de Musset.

while George waited worriedly at her desk for the sound of his returning footfalls on the flagstones.

One morning he came home covered with blood after a casual street fight, drunk to the point of incoherency and on the edge of delirium. Alarmed, George called in an Italian doctor. He declared that the poet, who had fallen prey to another spell, was dangerously ill. In the next days, Musset tossed feverishly—wild-eyed, racked, often violent. Sometimes he shrieked in terror at the hallucinations which gripped him. Sometimes he clutched at George with the desperate strength only the mad possess, so that it took two powerful men to loosen his grip on her.

During Musset's illness, the doctor—Pietro Pagello —came to visit frequently. He gave what medical help he could to his patient and often sat for hours with George at Musset's bedside. After many anxious days, the crisis passed and Musset settled into feeble conva- lescence. Gradually, as his strength returned, he seemed to feel that George, the self-sacrificing, minis- tering angel who had helped save his life, was once again the beautiful and extraordinary woman he had loved—and unfortunately rejected. What helped re- awaken the poet's appreciation of her was the love George appeared to have inspired in the young Italian doctor. With his pleasant, fresh face, his pink cheeks, his tendency toward plumpness, Pietro Pagello was not the sort of figure who would ordinarily attract the ro- mantic George, Musset knew. Yet the doctor's kindness and his untiring devotion to his patient had over- whelmed the poet himself. Now he began to wonder, had these same traits inspired George to return

Pagello's affection?

When he put this question to her, George replied that since Musset had rejected her, he no longer had the right to cross-examine her about her behavior; she was free to act as she chose. Before he had met her, Musset had lived by the "double standard," denying women the right to place their rejected emotions elsewhere while considering it perfectly natural for men to do so. Now, reluctantly, he accepted her answer. He left Venice, though not before all three had assured each other honestly and genuinely of their mutual friendship.

George accompanied Musset, still weak from his illness, as far as Mestre. As his ship disappeared down the lagoon toward the sea, she turned away despairingly. She was virtually penniless in a foreign country. She could not leave until she had finished her work and had received funds from her editor to pay for her own return home. She still loved Musset, though she would not admit it to herself. When the poet had rejected her, "a sharp, fierce love of life seized me, like an access of rage, in the midst of despair," she later wrote. And she thought she was strong enough now, the way she felt a man would be strong enough, to love another.

For four months, at any rate, she tried. She and Pietro Pagello moved into a tiny two-story house on a canal near the Ponte dei Barcarolli. Pietro shared the top floor with his brother Roberto and George the ground floor with the Pagellos' half sister Giulia. From his meager savings, Pietro bought secondhand furniture. In the evenings, George upholstered it with fresh material and sewed curtains, while Pietro sat improvising on an upright piano or Roberto strummed his guitar. Sometimes

Roberto would glance up at the Frenchwoman in puzzlement. She was drawn, frail, almost emaciated after her sleepless nights at Musset's sickbed, and Roberto would wonder what his brother saw in *questa sardella*, "this sardine."

But Pietro adored George. The tall young Italian doctor towered over her protectively. He considered the long hours she spent at her writing desk sacred. He tended to her every wish; he was considerate of her every mood. George had never received such attentions from Musset and she responded. Her hand lost in Pietro's great grip, she explored Venice with him, enjoying his company and that of his Italian friends. She enjoyed the trips she made with him to the towns of northern Italy. Most of all, perhaps, she enjoyed her work. She produced an incredible amount even for the prolific writer she was, sending off to Paris not only *Jacques*, the novel she had promised Buloz, but another novel and a novelette as well.

Meanwhile, anxious to return home to see her children, she dispatched a messenger daily to the General Delivery window at the post office to discover if the money had arrived. Mysteriously, it hadn't and, as the months passed, George was reduced to a penury unknown to her. She could not borrow from Pagello; poor himself, he would go out early in the morning, before his medical rounds, to the fields beyond the city to collect flowers for George because he could not afford to buy them. She ate less, bought only the barest necessities, and she kept on working.

But if the post brought her no mail from Buloz, it brought other letters from Paris which spoke of the scandal surrounding her and Musset. People were accusing her, she learned, of being an ogress who devoured men. She tried not to let this upset her and she wrote a friend, "If someone asks you what you think of the ferocious Lélia, just answer that she does not live on seawater and men's blood." But when she learned that Musset's behavior toward her was also the object of scandalous accusations, she instantly came to his defense.

She began a series of informal letters about her travels, which she entitled *Lettres d'un voyageur* (*Letters of a Traveller*). She sent the first three to Musset, asking him to pass them on to her editor if he approved. She addressed herself affectionately in them to an unknown correspondent, but one whom the literary world of Paris in 1834 could not mistake for anyone but Alfred de Musset. Buloz, who published them, felt these letters contained some of the finest writing George had ever done—a judgment corroborated by posterity. George wrote Musset, "I saw in them a pretext to speak aloud of my tenderness for you and to seal once and for all the lips of those who would not fail to say that you have ruined me and abandoned me."

Musset's reaction to the scandal mirrored hers. "It makes not the slightest difference to me," he wrote when he heard that people "are vomiting all they have in their entrails against me." But he was outraged at the insults leveled at George and promised her that he would write a novel rescuing her character, even if in doing so he would have to assassinate his own—"I shall build an altar to you, if need be, of my bones."

These two, whose "minds in their elevated sphere," as the poet wrote, had "recognized each other like two mountain birds and flown toward one another," did not remain apart for long. The money from Buloz had been languishing for months in the wrong slot at the post office; when it was at last discovered by a clerk, and George was able to leave Italy, Pagello accompanied her. Musset himself, out of concern for George's safety on the journey, had urged him to do so. But the Italian doctor soon went back home, aware that he had no real place in her life. Though George retired to Nohant to be with her children, and Musset went to Germany, the two were in Paris again within a short time. Once more the poet came to the blue attic on the quai Malaquais and did not leave.

Almost from the start, however, Musset grew fiercely jealous of George's past with Pagello. He began to reproach her, first in a lighthearted way, then with increasing anger and bitterness. At times he was so insulting that he became appalled at his own cruel tongue and, breaking down, begged her forgiveness. But no sooner were they reconciled than Musset began to torment George with new jealous rages. Their life together became "a long agony." Musset suffered because George refused to lie "like a coquettish woman" about her relationship with Pagello. George suffered from the bewildering contrasts in the poet's dual nature which forced her to write: "Why did you love me again after hating me? What mysterious change takes place in you with each passing week? Why this crescendo of displeasure, disgust, aversion, fury, cold and contemptuous mockery, then suddenly those tears, that sweetness, that ineffable love which comes flooding back!"

Musset could explain it neither to her nor to himself. He could not even justify his contrite moods. "Just because you weep, do you think that makes you innocent?" he later demanded of himself when he wrote of this period. "Nero wept too, when he killed his mother. . . . You are capable of striking a mortal blow and afterward, like Brutus, engraving upon your sword the chatter of Plato! You plunge this blistering weapon into the heart of a human being who opens her arms to you. You bear the mortal remains of your passion to the cemetery to scatter over the tomb the sterile flowers of your pity. And you say to passersby, 'What do you expect of me? I was taught to kill, and please observe that I am crying over my deed and that God has made a better man of me.' You give youth as your excuse, you believe that heaven will pardon you . . . and you argue it out through long nights of insomnia in the hopes that your soul will at last be granted a little peace."

In search of peace herself, George fled to Nohant to try to live without Musset, though she still loved him desperately. When she could bear their separation no longer, she hastened back to Paris. She was stunned to discover that Musset's friends had convinced him that he must never see her again, insisting that his violent love for her was destroying him. He ceased to respond to George's letters and broke off all contact with her.

George was overwhelmed by a melancholy she had never experienced before—so intense at moments that it drove her to thoughts of suicide. Unable to work for the first time in her life, she poured out her pain and longing into her *Journal intime* (*Intimate Journal*) . . . a kind of diary which took the form of letters. She addressed them to Musset, but she did not mail them. She did not suspect that one day these tortured and tender effusions would find an enduring place in French romantic literature.

"O, blue eyes that will look into mine no longer," ran one entry. "Fair face that I shall never see tilting over me with sweet languor . . . farewell. Farewell to all that I loved and that once was mine. Now when I burn at nights with passionate fire, I will embrace the trunks of pine trees and the rocks in the forest crying out your name, and then, having dreamed of pleasure, fall senseless to the damp earth. . . ."

During this period, good friends tried to console her, among them Franz Liszt, the Hungarian pianist and composer. From the age of nine, Liszt had dazzled audiences with his superlative technique at the keyboard. Now, in his early twenties—extraordinarily handsome, with blond hair that fell below his ears, and pale, delicate, beautiful hands—he was captivating listeners in the salons and concert halls of Paris. Music lovers regarded this astonishing virtuoso—who was the first performer to play an entire evening of solos without the aid of other musicians and without the music before him—as the greatest pianist who had ever lived. A romantic himself, if a deeply religious one, Liszt admired George

Franz Liszt. Portrait by Ary Scheffer.

Sand and her writings. One night, touched by her sufferings, he sat with her until two in the morning. "Only
God deserves to be loved" as she loved, he told her.
Though George appreciated his sympathy, she drew
little comfort from his words. "When one has loved a
man, it is so hard to love God, it is so different," she
wrote wistfully.

The *Revue des Deux Mondes* needed a portrait of
George and sent her to the studio of the great Romantic
painter Eugène Delacroix. During one of the sittings,
he gave her what she considered good counsel. "Give
in to your feelings," he told her. "When I am in such
a state, I do not act proud, I was not born a Roman. I
abandon myself to despair. It eats at me, it crushes me,
it kills me. When it has had enough, it grows weary and
it leaves me."

George asked herself in her diary that night, "But will
mine ever leave me? It only increases every day. . . ."
Finally she grew so desolate that in an attempt to reach
Musset's heart, she took scissors to the long dark hair
he adored and sent it to him. The poet forgot all his
friends' warnings and rushed to her side.

Once again, they were swept up in a troubled passion
in which, as Sainte-Beuve wrote, "they curse one another, rediscover one another, tear each other apart,
suffer." Unable to watch the mutual destruction of two
human beings he cherished, neither of whom appeared
capable of giving in to the other, Sainte-Beuve pressed
George to make a final break with Musset. Late in February of 1835, she wrote the poet: "I have loved you,
and I still bleed with this love. I pity you, I forgive you
everything, but we must part. Sainte-Beuve is right."

George Sand, after she took scissors to her long hair and sent the shorn locks to Alfred de Musset. Painting by Eugène Delacroix.

Musset answered that he himself would leave Paris—he had already reserved a seat on the mail coach to Strasbourg—he begged only for one last meeting. But George took the initiative. When Musset arrived at the quai Malaquais, she was gone. Musset walked away from the blue attic that day and never returned.

George and Musset saw each other afterward on only rare occasions . . . notably one night several years later when they met briefly in the crowd at the Paris Opéra, after which he wrote his nostalgic love poem "Souvenir." His relationship with George, however, left a lasting mark upon Musset and inspired more than one of his works. In his novel *La Confession d'un enfant du siècle* (*The Confession of a Child of the Century*), he built for George the "altar" he had promised. He lauded the independent spirit, courage and moral strength of a heroine he described as a painter and whose name was Brigitte, but who in all other respects was George Sand.

George herself wrote a novel in which she treated the poet's divided nature with sensitivity and penetration. She built her own sort of altar, not only to his genius —which she considered far superior to her own—but to the ideal they had pursued in the rare marriage of minds and hearts they had achieved for a little while. She called the book *Elle et Lui* (She and He). It was only in 1859, however, shortly after Musset's death, and when she had attained sufficient serenity to think of him without fear of reopening old wounds, that she saw the book into print. But such was not at all the state of mind —this early March day in 1835—of the distracted and heartsore woman who had packed up a bag in secret and fled the quai Malaquais.

7

Back at Nohant once again, George felt "sad but calm." To her mentor, Sainte-Beuve, she wrote, "I have done what I had to do, late it is true, but I have done it in the right way." And to her editor Buloz: "I am working. In five or six days you will have a story called *Mauprat*." Her inner turmoil was reflected in an illness which covered her with sores from head to foot. Though her children were in boarding school in Paris, where she had been able to visit them frequently, she had to forego seeing them for the moment. She was determined not to go near the capital for fear of meeting Musset.

Her self-imposed exile in the country was particularly unpleasant. Casimir had not changed; he still caroused over the bottle, still took up with village girls and servant maids. He reigned on the "domestic throne" with an absolute authority which made George feel that "neither my house nor my children belonged to me." The former army officer in him disapproved of his wife's indulgent attitude to self-willed Solange and to sensitive, artistic Maurice. He preferred strict, if sometimes heartless, discipline. He refused to listen to any suggestion George made for extricating Nohant from the financial ruin which his rash handling of the estate was bringing about. He told the servants not to obey his wife's orders.

George found her position intolerable, and she

sought help from Alexis Duteil, a lawyer in La Châtre, a friend of hers but especially of Casimir's. He told her that she could only become mistress of Nohant if she became Casimir's mistress. But it seemed to George that "a woman who tries to seduce her husband in order to make him submit to her will can only be compared to a prostitute earning her bread," and she knew she would have to find another solution.

She thought she had discovered one when Casimir decided that he wanted to leave Nohant and its burdensome financial problems behind him to live a free bachelor's life in the capital . . . on the revenues from a town house which had been part of his wife's inheritance. He signed an agreement which divided George's property between them, and she willingly signed it too; though it would deprive her of half her inheritance, it would leave her in full possession of her childhood home. The agreement was to come into effect in November. In the meantime, George wanted to get as far away as possible from Nohant—and from Casimir—and she planned a journey to the Middle East.

But almost immediately Casimir regretted what he considered an immense sacrifice on his part. He began to complain so bitterly to their mutual friends of the loss of what he called his "little empire" at Nohant that George tore up the agreement and sent the shreds to Duteil, writing, "My role in life is to be free, my inclination to accept favors from no one, not even when the charity is paid for with my own money." But this proud stand left her exactly where she had been before. Rankling anew in her role of an unwanted boarder whose presence irritated her husband, George allowed herself to be persuaded to seek the help of one of the cleverest lawyers in France. He happened to be living less than eighty miles away, in the town of Bourges. His name was Louis-Chrysostome Michel, though he was always called simply Michel de Bourges.

His father had been a woodcutter, a republican who had been murdered by a band of royalists. Raised as a peasant, Michel still proudly guarded traces of his humble origins in the shaggy coat and wooden shoes he wore, though he fastidiously wore as well the finest of silk shirts. He had been driven by powerful ambition to become not only an eminent lawyer at the age of thirty-seven, but an adored leader of the republican movement in France. He led a sober life, drinking nothing stronger than sugar water with his meals, but he was such an intellectual firebrand, exhausting himself continuously in impassioned debate, that his body was racked by chronic illnesses. Poor health had turned him prematurely bald, hollowed the flesh between the granite features of his pale face and lent a solemn, sepulchral timbre to his voice. He had great personal magnetism, however, and people said that when he was caught up in one of his astonishing flights of words he seemed almost handsome.

George and two of her Berrichon friends met in Bourges, settled in at the local inn, then invited the famous lawyer to visit them. Michel de Bourges had just read *Lélia* and his enthusiasm—intense as were all his emotions—caused him to hasten over to meet its author. The immediate object of George's journey was dispensed with briefly; he agreed to help her when and if she decided to take legal proceedings against Casimir for the repossession of Nohant. What interested this violent radical much more—and George, too, she discovered—was his outrage over George's skeptical attitude towards politics.

"I had always regarded current events with a cool eye," she wrote later. "I had looked upon the thousand accidental happenings of contemporary history, which surged around me like a swollen and troubled river, and had said to myself, *I'm not drinking that water.*"

But Michel de Bourges took her to task over the dinner table that evening at the inn. Her concern for liberty, he told her, was only a selfish concern for her own precious individual liberty, and she had no thought for the freedom of the oppressed millions who were her fellow members of the human race. While they suffered, she spent her time looking for some kind of abstract perfection. He even went so far, in his radical fervor, as to say that she and her intellectual breed would be justifiably beheaded in some future social revolution.

The charming head of the celebrated authoress seemed to have bewitched the lawyer all the same, for he broke all his own records for eloquence. After dinner the little group promenaded through the deserted streets of Bourges and Michel talked until four in the morning. George was impressed by his extraordinary intellectual powers. Whether his arguments impressed her was another matter. She was too exhausted to know. She wanted time to think, and the next day she left Bourges without even bidding him good-bye.

But Michel gave George no respite. No sooner had she arrived back in Nohant than she received a long letter "burning with the same breath of proselytism which I thought he had spent during our night wander-ings." As one letter followed another so rapidly that there was no time for George to answer them, it became clear to her that "this ardent mind had resolved to capture mine. All its faculties were strained toward that end." George was not at all ready to see her indepen-dent mind fall under the sway of another's. But Michel's words had piqued her, and when an important political trial began in Paris, in which Michel was participating as a defense lawyer, she decided to attend it as an ob-server.

It was a mass trial of one hundred twenty-one men who, early in April 1835, had joined in an insurrection against King Louis-Philippe. The insurrection had begun in the city of Lyons, where some thirty thousand weavers lived in abject poverty and worked sixteen hours a day in the textile factories. Their children worked too, never leaving the factories even at night, eating and sleeping beside the looms. When the weav-ers had asked for a raise in wages and been refused, they had taken to the streets, demanding not only higher wages, but also a republican government with democratic rights. In a matter of days, the weavers' uprising had spread to workers in other cities in France. It had then been ruthlessly suppressed by the king's guns and its leaders indicted by the courts.

The outcome of this Monster Trial, as it was called, was a foregone conclusion—no mercy could be ex-pected for the insurrectionists—yet radical intellectuals flocked to Paris to defend them and their republican ideas. A well-known Christian socialist, the Abbé Féli-cité de Lamennais, was there in the threadbare coat and woolen stockings of a country priest. The eminent chemist François Raspail was present, too, along with many prominent republican leaders. Women were not permitted in the visitors' gallery, but George disguised herself as a man and brazened her way past the ushers to attend some of the sessions of the trial. At night heated political discussions took place when Michel de Bourges brought his fellow members of the defense committee to her apartment on the quai Malaquais. "Within a few days," George wrote, "my whole life changed totally."

But though her sympathies were awakened to the republican cause and she became intrigued by the political issues raised at the trial, George did not embrace Michel de Bourges' revolutionary ideas. Instead, she maddened the lawyer constantly by clinging serenely to her own romantic view of life.

One night when they were walking with some friends along the banks of the Seine and, as usual, talking politics, they paused near a bridge. Courtly dance music was drifting toward them from the royal palace of the Tuileries across the river. Michel and the others were discussing the notion of a future society in which private property would be abolished. George broke in to comment that it was an untimely notion which would hardly lead people to advance toward a new civilization.

"Civilization!" Michel exclaimed, striking his cane against the balustrade of the bridge. "Yes, that's a fine word for you artists—civilization! Well, let me tell you that this corrupt society of yours will be rejuvenated only when the river below us flows red with blood, when that cursed palace is reduced to ashes and this great city upon which you are gazing is leveled to virgin soil over which the poor can drive their plows and build their homes."

He began to speak of that new golden age and of the social paradise which he believed would one day be constructed by man. When he broke off, George sighed. "For hours you have been pleading the cause of death with the voice of a Dante returning from hell. Now that I am enjoying your pastoral symphony, why do you stop?"

"The only things that interest you are words, phrases, images," Michel retorted. "You listen to me as if I were a poem or an orchestra, nothing more. You are not in the least convinced!"

It was partially true. Though George had been temporarily caught up that night by Michel's eloquence and had been "conquered by a keen desire to share those life-giving hopes for a society reborn," the next morning she woke up feeling "as if I had fallen from heaven back down to earth." And, with a shrug of her shoulders, she decided after all to take the trip she had planned and "go off to search for flowers and butterflies in Egypt or in Persia."

When Michel arrived at the quai Malaquais, he found George with her passport in her hand. She announced to him: "I've had enough of your republics. All of you have a republic which isn't mine and which isn't even the same for any one of you. You are getting nowhere. I will come back and applaud you when you have worn out your utopias and have managed to collect some sensible ideas."

Michel replied that she was acting like a "demanding

and brainless schoolchild. One day you don't want to know anything—the next you want to know everything. *Quick, quick, reveal God's secrets to Mr. George Sand who doesn't wish to be kept waiting!* Well, I have discovered something about you—you cannot reason, you can only feel."

George wondered if Michel could be right. Though he had attacked one of her most sacred beliefs—the supremacy of the heart over the mind—she somehow did not want to stop him as he went on to attack still another:

> You dream of personal freedom. You say that now you belong to yourself heart and soul. But there is a danger-ous fallacy in that. Total freedom cannot be reconciled with social responsibility. Just imagine—if all those who loved the truth were to turn their backs, as you are doing now, on their country, on their brothers, on their task on earth, then truth would not have one single cham-pion. It does not mount on the saddle of people who gallop off in flight. It is not to be found in solitude or on mountaintops.

For several moments George remained lost in thought. When she raised her eyes to answer Michel, she discovered that he had gone. He had even locked the door behind him. She decided that he had taken the key simply out of absentmindedness. But when the law-yer returned three hours later, he told George that he had locked her in on purpose. He had been expected at a meeting. Realizing that he had not yet convinced her, he had wanted to give her time for reflection.

"Now that you have thought things over," he said, "here is your key, the key to freedom!"

"No. I was wrong," she said. "I am staying. . . ."

In the days that followed, George grew more involved in the Monster Trial, and before long she had changed from observer to participant. The government had sidestepped legalities by creating an extraordinary court of law. The defense committee was seeking to challenge the court's right to try the accused. Michel asked George to draft a manifesto to that effect, and she set to work on it. She grew more interested, too, in men like the Abbé de Lamennais, whom Franz Liszt brought one evening to the quai Malaquais. Liszt, whose republicanism was a blend of mysticism and Romanticism, was one of the Abbé's most devout followers. The personality of the humble Breton priest, whom the Vatican had strongly censured for his liberal views, fascinated George. After Liszt performed his usual astonishing pyrotechnics on the piano that evening, George and her friends talked with the Abbé until the early hours of the morning about Christianity and socialism.

During this period, the *Revue des Deux Mondes* published another of George's now celebrated and popular *Lettres d'un voyageur*. It was number six of the series, and it was addressed to a man whom she called Everard, but who in real life was Michel de Bourges. Shaped from actual letters she had sent Michel, it revealed George's rapidly changing views:

I have lived so much but have done nothing worthwhile. Does anyone want to use my life, now or in the future? If only it can be made to serve an idea and not simply passion, serve the truth and not simply a man, I'll obey orders. I warn you, I can act but not make decisions, for I don't know anything and am certain of nothing. I can

Michel de Bourges. Drawing by Péronard.

be no more than a common soldier. Never mind! On-
ward! I don't care about the subtle differences on your
banners as long as your troops march forward along the
road to a republican future. In the name of Jesus . . . in
the name of Washington and Franklin who left their task
on earth unfinished—as long as some good can be done
and those who believe this can prove it—I'm only a stray
child loitering about the barracks, but take me with you.

For this letter, in which she had also indirectly referred to King Louis-Philippe as a "crowned log," and
for her close association with republican leaders, the
government soon ranked her with the "seditious" opposition and the police began to watch her movements.

But Michel found George's draft of the manifesto too
soft, still too full of humanitarian generalities, and he
rewrote it. His version, however, was considered too
revolutionary by more moderate members of the defense committee. After lengthy arguments, Michel was
forced to print the manifesto with only the partial support of the committee. When he defended his ideas
before the judges, they were outraged. They charged
him with contempt of court, fined him ten thousand
francs and sentenced him to a month in jail.

George stood by Michel, who fell seriously ill immediately after the court session. She helped to nurse
him back to health, and a few weeks before he was to
begin serving his prison sentence in Bourges, she took
him off to Nohant. The country house was deserted;
Casimir was away in Paris, where he had gone to fetch
Maurice for the summer holidays. George spent three
days with Michel in the shuttered house, emerging only
at night to walk along the garden paths by moonlight.

The servants were given orders to tell callers that no one was at home. When Michel was considered fit enough to begin his jail term, George traveled with him as far as Bourges, where he was imprisoned, then rode back alone to Nohant.

Casimir returned, and with him the tensions which had become chronic in this marriage-in-name-only. A few months before, Casimir had once more decided that he wanted to leave Nohant for good, had once more signed an agreement with George and now the time was approaching when it was to come into force. Meanwhile, Casimir had become more and more irritable. Torn between his desire to be free of Nohant and his reluctance to give it up, he took out his irritation on George. She loathed family bickering and when Casimir took to insulting her before servants and friends, she accepted this in silence. One evening, however, an unexpected incident occurred.

It was mid-October, and the end of a normal day at Nohant. Solange and Maurice were spending a few days with their parents. Some dozen friends had been invited to dine and after the meal were taking coffee in the parlor. Maurice was walking around and around his father's chair, and Casimir angrily commanded him to stop. Seeing that her husband was drunk, George sought to protect her twelve-year-old son, but this only deflected Casimir's anger toward her; he ordered her to leave the room. She refused, saying quietly that the house was hers as much as his. He flew at her to strike her, grabbing hold of her violently. Friends intervened, and the blow intended for George struck another. Casimir roared at them not to interfere—he was master in the house—and he ran to the room where he kept his hunting weapons and seized a gun. He was starting back toward George when suddenly he found the lawyer, Duteil, who had always been more his friend than his wife's, blocking his way.

Livid, Casimir allowed himself to be disarmed, and after a while he quieted down. But by now George had disappeared to her room. She came to a decision. She would not wait for the agreement she had signed with Casimir to come into effect; even though divorce was impossible in France, she would take the initiative and demand at least a legal separation.

She went to see a lawyer in La Châtre who, unlike Duteil, was her friend, not Casimir's. He agreed with her decision but suggested they consult with Michel as well, and they took off on the road to Bourges. When they reached the prison it was two in the morning, but they bribed a guard and were led to Michel's cell. Michel, too, agreed that legal proceedings should be started immediately but advised George not to return to Nohant; if she continued to live under the same roof as her husband, she might prejudice her case. When she left the prison, she drove straight to La Châtre and, though uncertain of her welcome, knocked on Duteil's door. Because of Casimir's behavior, Duteil's sympathies had shifted, and he promised George she could stay with him and his family until her case was decided.

In the nineteenth century, a legal separation between a husband and wife was almost always accompanied by a public scandal so damaging to the reputation of the woman involved that it was a step few women dared take. George hoped, however, that Casimir would not contest the case and that if she won by default, no publicity would be attached to it which could harm her or her children. And, indeed, in the early stages of the lawsuit, Casimir did not even bother to show up for the hearings at the district court. The judges, in accordance with the previously signed agreement, granted Nohant and the custody of the children to George.

But Casimir could not bear to see his wife's property slipping through his fingers. He challenged the decision of the lower courts and appealed the case to the royal court of Bourges. Now a public scandal was unavoidable and George had to prepare herself to face it. Yet, as she wrote her mother during this period: "I am my father's daughter and when my heart tells me that something is just, I don't care what the world has to say about it. If my father had listened to a lot of fools I would never have inherited his name. He left me a wonderful example of independence and parental devotion. I will follow it and rescue my children, even if I scandalize the whole universe."

But for all her brave words, George was worried. And as the months dragged on and Casimir set about collecting the most damaging evidence he could uncover about his wife's behavior, she began to fear that the royal court at Bourges would decide against her. In that event she resolved upon a rash act. With the loan of ten thousand francs, which she arranged in secret, she would escape with her children to America.

The day of the trial arrived. The courtroom was crowded with people come from La Châtre, from Paris, from Bordeaux. George wore a simple white dress with a lace collar and white hood. Casimir was there, too, along with a lawyer who began to plead on his behalf.

"Dare one take Mr. Dudevant's children from him and leave them to a mother who has revealed to the eyes of all her licentious life and immoral doctrines?" he asked the court. He then proceeded to read extracts from George's writings, including the "letter of confession" she had sent her husband over a decade earlier about her relations with Aurélien de Sèze, whom she had met in the Pyrenees mountains. The lawyer demanded that George beg her husband's pardon and resume her role as his obedient wife.

Then Michel de Bourges took the floor. Deftly employing the same piece of evidence—the letter concerning Aurélien de Sèze—he quoted other passages from it which proved that George had remained faithful to Casimir during those early years of her marriage. He pointed out that it was Casimir's adulterous behavior which had rendered Nohant unlivable for George. But the main point of his argument was the contradiction in Casimir's position. If indeed Casimir was seeking his wife's return under the marital roof, why was he making every possible effort to blacken her character? Why did he—Michel demanded of Casimir—claim her with one hand and with the other sink a dagger into her breast?

It was a question that puzzled even the judges, for after the two-day session was over, they were split five to five and no conclusion was reached. In the meantime, newspapers were filled with reports of the trial. Casimir, who had not expected to see his own follies paraded in public, became anxious to put a stop to the proceedings. He withdrew the appeal and George won the case. A final agreement was signed granting her full custody of Solange, authorization to have Maurice with her whenever he was not at school, and repossession of Nohant.

George traveled back to her childhood home with her daughter. First of all she rearranged the furniture as it had been in her grandmother's time, then she set about the difficult task of rehabilitating the almost bankrupt estate. She was heavily in debt as a result of her legal battle with Casimir. The logical way to extricate herself, of course, was by writing popular romantic novels . . . the kind which her editor Buloz would be eager to publish, and for which her growing numbers of readers would be eager to pay good money. But George had witnessed the Monster Trial in Paris and come to know Michel de Bourges and had discovered a new aim. From now on, she decided, she would write only books which contained progressive social messages. And though France was entering upon a period of increasing political repression, she gave no thought to the dangerous consequences this decision might have upon her purse and her career.

8

George turned thirty-two the summer of 1836. Thirteen-year-old Maurice, who adored his mother, had suffered acutely from the taunts of his fellow students during the trial. Now he and Solange were home for the holidays and nearby La Châtre was still rife with gossip. George wanted to spare the children, and in August she set off with them for Switzerland.

For some time Franz Liszt had been urging her to visit him there. He himself had retired to Geneva to escape unfriendly tongues, for he was living with the Countess Marie d'Agoult, who had left her husband for him. George was fond of Liszt, who like herself was a republican and longed to see a democratic government established in France. He had given concerts to help raise money for the striking workers of Lyons, and the unsatisfied dream of this man who played to the aristocracy of Europe was "music for the people." George was determined to be fond as well of the somewhat cool, somewhat haughty noblewoman whom her friend's heart had chosen. She was also determined to ignore the absence of Michel de Bourges, whom she had expected to accompany her but who had backed out at the last minute. She did her utmost to make the holiday a carefree adventure for everyone.

From the beginning there was a carnival spirit to the group who met in Chamonix in France after picking up stray friends along the way. They journeyed toward Switzerland across the border, trekking up the glaciers of Mont Blanc on donkeys and racing each other on foot over the mountainsides. In inns where they spent the night, they often shocked other visitors. Solange wore the same boy's outfit her mother had worn as a girl. George, smoking her cigar, sported a striking man's costume—flowing blue cravat, black redingote and white trousers—while Liszt looked unusual enough simply by virtue of his long blond hair. One night an Englishman, peering through his spectacles at the pianist, asked his neighbor in a loud voice who "that fellow" was. Liszt was delighted with the English word and from then on he referred to himself and Marie as "Mr. and Mrs. Fellows." George had a weakness for nicknames. Since she and Maurice had somewhat long noses, she took the French slang word for nose—*pif*—and dubbed herself and her children the "Piffoëls."

During the three weeks they were together, the "Fellows" and the "Piffoëls" divided their time between sightseeing and long philosophical discussion. In the evenings they met with other friends in Marie d'Agoult's apartment in Geneva. There they exchanged comic stories or drew caricatures of one another. But the room always fell silent when Liszt started for the piano. George would stretch out on the floor beneath his piano, as she had done as a child under her grandmother's strident harpsichord. It was the only place, she insisted, where she could feel truly "enveloped" by music. And Liszt would play one of his new compositions.

George returned to France in late September, but soon she was reunited in Paris with the "Fellows." They had settled into the Hôtel de France on the rue Laffitte, and George—who had given up the blue attic on the quai Malaquais—took temporary rooms for herself and the children in the same hotel. Marie d'Agoult created a salon there where Romantic artists and advanced thinkers of the day met informally for music and conversation. George found many familiar faces among them. There was the Abbé de Lamennais and the republican Pierre Leroux, who had been present during the Monster Trial. There was the young Swiss writer Charles Didier, who had fallen hopelessly in love with

George, as had a number of the male admirers who usually surrounded her. There was also the German lyric poet Heinrich Heine.

Heine was a Jew who had converted to Protestantism in order to obtain a law degree in his native Germany. But even this "entry ticket to European civilization," as he called it, had not enabled him to find work at home. He had emigrated to Paris, where he was contributing to Buloz's *Revue des Deux Mondes* and writing the poetry which would one day make him world famous. Some years back, he and George had formed a comradely friendship, and they addressed each other in their letters as "Dear Cousin." But there were others who attended Marie's salon whom George knew less well or was meeting for the first time—Victor Schoelcher, journalist and ardent critic of the African slave trade; Adam Mickiewicz, the Polish epic poet; and, among the composers, Hector Berlioz.

Nearly all of these intellectuals believed that art must not only please the senses, but be socially useful as well. For this they were dubbed by cynical critics the "humanitarians." George, for one, was proud of the label and soon found a means of justifying it. The Abbé de Lamennais had recently become editor of a liberal newspaper called *Le Monde,* and asked George to contribute, giving her free rein in the choice of subject matter. George turned her back on lucrative offers from well-established journals to write for the Abbé for next to nothing. She began a series of articles on the status of women in society. They took the form of letters of advice addressed to a fictitious, unmarried girl called Marcie.

When her *Lettres à Marcie* (Letters to Marcie) began to appear, the freethinking Abbé was somewhat dismayed. It had not occurred to him that the ideal of human equality he so fervently embraced should be extended to *women*. He noted uneasily the heated disputes the series was inspiring in salons all over Paris, and when George's third article appeared, he made some judicious cuts in her recommendation that divorce be made legal in France.

George wrote the Abbé a letter, protesting that no discussion of the "feminine question" could neglect the question of divorce. "No matter how I search for a remedy to the bitter injustices, the endless miseries, the violent discords which disrupt marriages, I find no other solution than the right to break and re-form the marital bond. Believe me," she urged, "I know this matter better than you, and just this once let the disciple speak: Master, in this realm there are paths which you have never trodden, abysses where my eyes have plunged while yours have been fixed on the heavens. You have lived with the angels, but I have lived with men and women and know how much suffering, how much sinning exist, and how vast is the need for a law which makes virtue possible."

But the Abbé grumbled nevertheless and, after writing a few more letters in the series, George quit *Le Monde*, because the paper did not after all give her freedom to express her ideas. She set to work to finish *Mauprat*, the story she had begun for her editor Buloz but which, under her prolific pen, had taken on the proportions of a novel. Running through its Romantic framework was George's conviction that corruption does not come from within a human being but is caused by the social conditions under which people live. When she finished *Mauprat*, she began *Les Maîtres mosaïstes* (*The Master Mosaic-Workers*), a novel set in Venice about two rival clans of skilled craftsmen. It tackled yet another aspect of what George saw as a corrupting influence in society, the pressure of commercial interests upon artists which tempts them to lower their artistic standards. She wrote the novel during the two summer months of 1837 which Liszt and Marie d'Agoult spent at Nohant.

Solange was in boarding school. Maurice had been ill and his mother had taken him home temporarily to study with a tutor. While George worked in her study and Marie wandered tranquilly among the old lime trees in the garden, the sound of Liszt's piano alternated with the song of the nightingales in the wooded countryside. Yet it was a turbulent two months for George emotionally. Despite the letters she and Michel exchanged, despite the journeys George took, galloping on horseback to one town or another between Bourges and Nohant to meet Michel, it had become increasingly clear to her that his consuming ambition to rise in the world meant more to him than she ever could. She decided not to see him again. She felt unhappy about it and helpless, yet, as always, she went on working.

She soon received news that her mother had suddenly fallen critically ill, and she hastened to her side. Sophie Dupin had come to visit at Nohant occasionally after her daughter's marriage, but she had always been happier in Paris. As she used to say to George, "I prefer the dusty trees and black gutters of the boulevards to your scary forests and those rivers where one is always in danger of drowning." But Sophie had nevertheless followed her daughter's career closely, "with alternate moods of joy and fury." She would read some insulting review and, rushing instantly to George, cover her with angry reproaches. When George would ask her if she had read the book in question, Sophie would answer that she hadn't and did not intend to! But then she would read it and, "overcome with a mother's blind adoration, declare it sublime and the critics abominable."

George had often visited Sophie in Paris. When she knocked on the door of her apartment, she always knew from the response in what mood she would find her changeable mother. If it was a good one, the answer to the familiar knock would be a joyful cry, "Ah! There's my Aurore." But if it was a bad mood, the same knock would be answered simply, "Who is there?"

"That *Who is there?* used to fall upon my breast like a stone," George wrote, for she still loved her mother "with an instinctive passion" that nothing could alter. Now she was grieved to see her lying in a rest home and on the threshold of death. But though Sophie was aware of her approaching end, she still held on to something of her old spunk. During one of her last days, she pulled George close to her and said, "I don't want the face of a priest around here, do you understand? If I have to go, I want everyone around me to be smiling. After all, why should I be afraid of meeting God? He can blame me for anything He likes, but never for not having loved Him enough—that I defy Him to do!"

Frédéric Chopin in 1838. Portrait by Eugène Delacroix.

After Sophie's death, George returned to the countryside. Nevertheless, she kept making trips back up to Paris. One man drew her there and for some time now she had been trying to persuade Liszt to bring him to visit her at Nohant. Although he put in an occasional appearance at Marie d'Agoult's salons, it was not there George met him, but in his own modest yet flower-filled apartment on the rue de la Chaussée d'Antin where she had been invited with Liszt in the autumn of 1836. He was the outstanding composer and remarkable pianist Frédéric Chopin.

Chopin, born in Poland of a French father and a Polish mother, had come to Paris in 1831. A frail, sensitive young man with ash blond hair and a physical beauty which rivaled Liszt's, he was ever reluctant to appear in public. Yet even the few concerts he had given had been sufficient to reveal his astonishing gifts. Members of the Polish aristocracy in the capital were in exile, as Chopin was, from their native land, which had fallen under the domination of its Russian, Prussian and Austrian neighbors. These Polish emigrés had sought him out as a piano instructor. But though he lived a frugal life, teaching and composing, Chopin had the inclinations of an aristocrat. He was infinitely courteous, fastidious to the tips of his immaculate white gloves, and basically conservative in politics.

Despite his aristocratic leanings, however, Chopin was idolized by the Romantic school. He had departed, as they had, from classical formalism. The sonata form dissolved under his fingers into something less defined, more loosely constructed—the rhapsody, the impromptu, the étude. A composition of Chopin's was not a finished canvas in the old classical sense, but more like a beautiful page torn out of a painter's sketchbook. There was another reason too for the reverence in which he was held. Since music did not tell a story as literature did, nor present concrete images to the eye as painting did, but called upon the imagination through intangible harmonies and melodies, it was held to be the most Romantic of all the arts. Composers in the Romantic nineteenth century were ranked higher than poets or painters, and Chopin—the most Romantic of all the Romantics—held a godlike position in the artistic world. The painter Eugène Delacroix, who came to know him well, adored him, and George, who had loved music ever since childhood, longed to know him better.

But the reserved and retiring young composer, who was six years George's junior, was a little put off by this creature in man's clothing. When she entered his drawing room that evening with Liszt, she was flamboyantly dressed, in his honor, in the colors of the Polish flag—white trousers, red sash, a jacket with bright red buttons. Shy, as she always was in strange company, she had hastily sought out a fireside seat where she withdrew behind her cigar smoke to chat with one of the other guests. It was primarily a musical evening and soon Liszt and Chopin were at the piano. Chopin took the bass, Liszt the treble, and the two gave a dazzling performance which left their audience breathless.

After his first encounter with George, Chopin is said to have asked a friend, "Is she actually a woman?" He was inclined to doubt it. He appeared to be somewhat bewildered by her. In any event, though he had met her at least twice toward the end of 1836 and it was now the winter of 1838, he still had not responded to her invitation to come to Nohant.

That winter George received another visitor, however, whom she had not seen for a long time—Balzac. Five years earlier, when George had broken with Jules Sandeau, Balzac had sided with Sandeau, even taken him under his wing and encouraged him to write. But Balzac, like George Sand a demon for work, had finally become discouraged by Sandeau's indolence. One day George received a note from him, saying that he was in the vicinity and would like to make a "pilgrimage to Nohant" to visit "the nightingale in her nest." George responded with an invitation. Balzac was pleased to find George, who was thirty-three now, little changed by the years. Despite the emotional upheavals she had undergone, he noted, there was not a single white hair in her dark tresses and her eyes shone with the same brilliant luster. During their long talks that often lasted from five in the evening till five the next morning, the two discussed (as Balzac later wrote) "the great questions of marriage and freedom . . . candidly, seriously, and with the sense of responsibility of worthy shepherds anxious over the fate of the human flock."

After a week's stay, Balzac left Nohant with the memory of a woman of great heart to whom he could talk as he would talk to a man. He left there too with an idea for a new book. George was too close a friend of Liszt's and Marie d'Agoult's to write the lovers' story, so she had given it to Balzac. He recreated it in a novel called *Béatrix*, in which not only Liszt and Marie figured, but George as well. Under the name of Camille Maupin, she was described by Balzac as a woman gifted with genius who led an exceptional life which could not be judged by ordinary standards.

George returned to Paris in the spring and began to see Frédéric Chopin again. At each meeting, the composer was increasingly struck by her sensitivity to music, by the blend of gentle protectiveness and quiet strength she possessed, and by her unusual kind of beauty. One night he recorded in his journal: "She watched me while I played. The music was a little melancholy—the 'Legends of the Danube'—but my heart seemed to dance with her as her eyes held mine in their gaze. What were they saying to me, those dark, those curious eyes? She was leaning on the piano and her fiery gaze engulfed me. My heart was captured! Since that day I have seen her twice. She loves me. . . . Aurore, what a charming name!"

Indeed, George had fallen in love and, strangely enough, with a man whose opinions were diametrically opposed to hers on almost every subject. But for all their intellectual differences, they were bound closely by a shared passion for music and for beauty. Into the remote world of the creative artist where he had always lived alone, Chopin brought George, trusting her as he had never trusted anyone. Whenever he played her some new work, he waited for her reaction. Whenever she spoke, he listened, glowing under her tender encouragement. As she grew to know him well, George was able to identify with him completely and to understand a "mind that was as sensitive as an open wound; the mere fold of a rose petal or the shadow of a fly could make it bleed."

Chopin's health was delicate, as well. He had the disquieting, persistent cough associated with consumption, or tuberculosis—a disease which often proved fatal in the nineteenth century. George refused to regard his illness as anything more serious than chronic bronchitis. Still, as spring turned to summer and then summer to fall, she grew anxious for Chopin to spend the winter months in a warmer climate. Friends persuaded her that she would find an inexpensive, sunny paradise on the island of Majorca off the coast of Spain, and George seized upon the idea. Before they left for Majorca, however, they had to find money to pay for the trip.

Camille Pleyel was noted for the concerts he promoted in his Salons Pleyel in Paris and for the pianos he manufactured which bore his name. Chopin made an arrangement with him to compose twelve preludes in the major keys and twelve preludes in the minor keys for the sum of two thousand francs. For her part, George approached Buloz, who was not at all pleased with the direction her writing had been taking. The editor found her latest novel, *Spiridion*, altogether too high minded and didactic, but still he hoped her insistence upon a "social message" was only a passing phase, and he gave her a cash advance on future works.

In mid-October George and the children set off for the south of France by riverboat to meet Chopin not far from the Spanish border. From Port Vendres they journeyed by steamer to Barcelona and then on to the island of Majorca.

Throughout the journey, which took many days, the skies were blue, the sun was hot. Chopin was thrilled by the climate while Maurice, who had been pale and sickly during the past year, quickly began to turn into a healthy boy again. Even the spirited and contrary Solange, ever a bundle of trouble to her mother and to Maurice, seemed docile. She had been seasick on the voyage; as her brother said, she had lost all her "venom" along with her meals.

The little family settled into a rented house, poorly furnished, but their backyard was a mountainside covered with pine and olive groves, while before them stretched the turquoise Mediterranean. Chopin immediately sat down to an out-of-tune rented piano and began to work on his preludes. George put out her ink and pens. At the same time she unpacked a trunk filled with schoolbooks and started Maurice and Solange on their lessons. "What a sky! What a landscape! We're in ecstasy," she wrote back to Paris. In his letters the composer's enthusiasm matched hers.

Soon, however, the southern sun disappeared behind clouds and the island began to be whipped by cold gales from the sea. Weeks of driving rain followed. Chopin's cough grew worse and he began spitting blood. The Spanish doctors recommended bleeding. The treatment involved drawing blood from a vein; this was held a cure at that time for almost any ailment which baffled medical science. But George knew that bleeding was dangerous for a man with a frail constitution and she forbade it. Instead she began to cook special meals for Chopin, whose delicate stomach could not digest Spanish cooking, and she ordered another stove to heat the damp, cold house.

But word spread in the village that Chopin had consumption—a disease considered so contagious that, by Spanish law, any bed that a consumptive had slept in had to be burned. The landlord took fright and not only evicted his tenants but made them pay for the cost of repainting and replastering his contaminated walls as well as replacing the beds.

The members of the Chopin-Sand household began to be treated as pariahs by the local population. People shrank from the touch of Chopin's hand, and beds were burned behind them wherever they stayed. They were forced to seek refuge in a deserted monastery on a mountaintop at Valldemosa. For many weeks they lived there in the vaulted cells beneath foggy skies where the sound of swooping buzzards mingled with the notes from Chopin's piano . . . at first a rented one, but later one Camille Pleyel had shipped to him from Paris. George did her own work, encouraged Chopin in his, taught the children their lessons, helped with the sweeping and cooking, and bought a goat and a sheep to provide the composer with milk, which she had to mix with ground almonds to make palatable. She was tough-minded enough to bear the hard work, the solitude, and the fierce hostility of the Spaniards toward this "heathen" family who refused to attend Mass. But when she saw that Chopin was growing depressed by their isolation, haunted by visions of dead monks, and convinced that he would never leave Valldemosa alive, she decided to take him away.

In late February George, Chopin and the children arrived in the south of France again. By this time, winter and the arduous journey had so weakened Chopin that to move further might have endangered his life. They

The Monastery at Valldemosa.

In an orange grove in Majorca, Maurice and Solange "stuff
themselves sick with oranges." Drawing by Maurice Sand.

spent three months in Marseilles, while he recovered his strength. George kept on working, and Chopin's admiration for her talent and industry was boundless. He wrote a Polish friend in Paris that his "angel" had turned out a "superb article on Goethe, Byron and Mickiewicz." And, in the next letter, he proudly announced that she was already in the throes of a new novel, adding, "You would love her still more if you knew her as I do now."

By late spring Chopin was at last able to continue the journey northward, and on June first their carriage rolled into the courtyard at Nohant. That summer Chopin settled into George's country home, where he began to compose mazurkas, sonatas and nocturnes which would later become famous throughout the world. Chopin took discreet care to refer to George as his "hostess" whenever he spoke or wrote of her to his friends. Nevertheless, he was a fully accepted member of the family. Though he was hopeless in practical matters and lived for the most part in a world of his own, the children had grown fond of him. In the evenings he sat playing four-handed music with Solange or admired a new drawing by Maurice. The sixteen-year-old boy had decided to become an artist and had brought back with him an album full of sketches he had done in Majorca. On occasion Chopin would discuss music with Delacroix, who later became a frequent visitor and who painted in an attic studio George kept available for him. Often Chopin entertained the household with brilliant comic imitations at the piano of noted musicians of the day, or he took part in the pantomimes and amateur theatricals he inspired.

When winter came, Chopin returned to Paris to earn money as a piano instructor. George and the children accompanied him to the capital. They lived first on separate streets, then in the same building on the rue Pigalle and, later, on the sunny and spacious square d'Orléans where they moved into two separate apartments. They chose this arrangement not only because Chopin wanted to keep up appearances for the sake of his strict Catholic family back in Poland, but also because they led such different lives.

Chopin mingled with the aristocracy and gave piano lessons to their children. Among his friends were the Polish Princess Czartoryska, the Countess Potocka, the wealthy Rothschilds. George mingled with radical thinkers like Pierre Leroux, and with poets and philosophers of the working class. But Chopin and she were closely linked emotionally and in the realm of music. Their opposing sympathies in other spheres seemed secondary to them. Sometimes Chopin would come home from a private performance for the King and Queen, their murmured praises of "Divine!" or "Delicious!" still ringing in his ears and bearing the royal gift of a gilded silver cup in his hand. He would find George at her desk penning a letter of encouragement to a locksmith or a mason on his latest proletarian verses. George and Chopin always tried to be tolerant of each other's views, and George was especially careful to avoid violent clashes of ideas. She was afraid of their effect upon his temperament and delicate health.

Summer found the family back at Nohant. Chopin missed the social whirl of Paris but his cough improved in the clean country air and he spent his days working.

There was a piano in the salon on the garden floor, and later a small upstairs room adjacent to Chopin's bedroom was converted into a music room. To the other side of his bedroom, which was decorated with bright Chinese wallpaper, was a book-filled study . . . and then George's room. While she wrote, she could hear Chopin composing. Sometimes a folk theme of the native Poland he loved and whose lost liberty he constantly mourned would be transformed instantly into a defiant polonaise. But he was often tortured and dissatisfied, George recalled in her memoirs, and "would close himself up in his room for days, pacing up and down, breaking his quills, playing the same measure over and over again, changing it a hundred times. He would write it down, rub it out, write it down, rub it out, then the next day start anew with a meticulous and desperate perseverance. He spent six weeks on one page, only to return to what he had written in the first flight of inspiration."

George and Chopin lived under the same roof for eight years. Early on, the composer's ill health and his often alarming fragility led George to impose a sexual abstinence which Chopin reluctantly accepted and which transformed their union into a profound, tender, loving friendship. When at times Chopin's racking cough made him too weak to leave his bed and he lay there filling handkerchiefs with the blood he spat up, George nursed him devotedly. If on occasion her troublesome liver made her ill, he in turn nursed her with the same devoted care. Chopin encouraged George by his admiration for her work, which she read aloud to him in the evenings. She was not a passive witness to his creative suffering but tried to help him trust in that first "flight of inspiration."

One night, a visitor to Nohant recalled, George was carried away by her love for nature and was talking about the tranquil countryside around them. Chopin was struck by her words.

"What you've been saying just now is beautiful," he commented.

"Do you think so?" she returned. "Well then, put it into music."

George knew that nature's sounds could not be literally transposed. She was not suggesting the "imitative harmony" Chopin disdained, but the "sublime equivalent in musical thought." The composer sat down at the piano and began to make up a kind of pastoral symphony at the keyboard. George was standing behind him, watching the light play on those skilled, delicate hands where at times she had seen something approaching the pallor of death. She laid her own hand gently on his shoulder murmuring, "Keep up your courage, velvet fingers. . . ."

While Chopin went on composing and giving piano lessons, George's professional life became fraught with difficulties. Displeased though Buloz was with her didactic novels, he had nevertheless published them. But when George sent him the manuscript of *Le Compagnon du tour de France* (*The Companion of the Tour of France*), he was dismayed by its direct attack upon the wealthy upper classes. Considering it far too radical for his conservative journal, he demanded that George make changes. She refused. Buloz refused to publish it. When the novel appeared nevertheless—for she took it to another publisher—reviewers were violent in their criticism. One of them not only vilified the novel for its radical content but vilified George personally, claiming that she had the habit of going to the working-class districts on Sundays and getting drunk with "the People."

George soon answered these critics with a novel even more forthright in its radicalism. When Buloz read her *Horace*, he was thoroughly shocked; in romantically ideal terms, it called for the eventual abolition of private property. He could find no other label for George now than "communist." It was clear to both George and Buloz that after almost a decade of professional association they could not possibly work together any longer. The final break was painful on both sides but especially for George, for when her contract with the *Revue des Deux Mondes* was dissolved, she found herself in even more desperate financial straits. She owed Buloz a considerable sum of money for advances on stories that now he would not print. But as George wrote him, "I am willing to ruin myself, provided I can write what I think."

The problem, of course, was to find a publisher who would be willing to print what she wrote. But the conservative mood in the country was reflected in the publishing world, and George decided that the only solution was to create a new radical review. Under the editorship of the republican Pierre Leroux, and the management of a liberal journalist, Louis Viardot, and with a promise from George that she would provide material regularly, the new radical *Revue indépendante* was launched. The first issue contained the opening installment of *Horace* and an article by George on proletarian poets.

Although *Horace* was received indifferently by the public, the circulation of the magazine increased when George began to serialize a new novel in it called *Consuelo*. This romantic story, with its vast canvas of fictional characters and real historical figures, became so popular that, after writing one hundred fifty chapters, George was forced to extend it with a sequel called *La Comtesse de Rudolstadt* (*The Countess of Rudolstadt*). The heroine of the novel was inspired by a dear friend of George's and Chopin's, the great mezzo-soprano Pauline Viardot.

But working under pressure and for little money took its toll on George's health. An optic nerve became so inflamed that she suffered fierce migraines and had to wear dark glasses to protect her sight. Even so, she was less concerned with her own than with Chopin's health, which was declining as each winter passed. For some time now the composer himself had suspected the gravity of his condition. "They tell me I am getting better," he wrote one night in his diary, "but I sense deep inside me that something is wrong. Aurore's eyes are sad. They shine only when I play. My fingers glide softly over the keys, her pen flits across the page. She can write while listening to music. Music above her, all around her, Chopin's music, sweet but as bright as words of love. For you, Aurore, nothing is too much for me. I would give you all I possess. I want to live for you alone. . . ."

Unfortunately, George could not say the same to Chopin—too many others depended on her. Her children were now grown up, but she was their sole support. She had adopted as well a cousin on her mother's side, a penniless young girl called Augustine Brault who was a few years older than Solange. In addition there were continuous drains on her purse brought about by her unfailing generosity. She helped poverty-stricken poets, writers, philosophers, and she helped the villagers in Nohant too. She was obliged to write book after book without pausing to rest.

La Mare au diable (*The Devil's Pool*), written during this period, has become a classic, while *Lucrezia Floriani* is remembered primarily for the penetrating portrait it reveals of Frédéric Chopin. Chopin did not recognize himself in the character of the handsome Prince Karol —an intolerant and pathologically jealous man. Yet, after nearly eight years with George, this was in fact what the ever more ailing composer was becoming. With each relapse in his health, "his thoughts turned blacker and gloomier." He grew so possessive of her that he resented George's friends. He even resented the attention she lavished on Maurice and Solange, though he was deeply attached to them.

One day Chopin, whom Maurice had always adored, wounded Maurice's feelings "in an unexpected way on an inconsequential matter," as George recalled in her memoirs. "They embraced the next minute, but the grain of sand had fallen into the peaceful lake and little by little stones began to fall one after another." Maurice was going on twenty-four and, "weary of pinpricks" Chopin was inflicting on him, spoke of leaving home. George interfered, saying she would not allow it, whereupon Chopin "lowered his eyes and murmured that I loved him no longer." The composer announced that he himself would leave and George did nothing to stop him; perhaps a few months away from her, she hoped, would cure him of his sick jealousy. Chopin went off to Paris without realizing that he would never see Nohant again.

A few months later, George moved back to the square d'Orléans. She and Chopin met, they went to a Delacroix exhibit together, they found something of their old "calm friendship." It was a friendship they both treasured. And they might have held on to it longer if not for the interference of third parties . . . people only too willing to hurt George by destroying her image in Chopin's eyes. One of these was George's daughter.

At the age of nineteen, Solange was a headstrong, golden-haired beauty. She had precipitously married a man she scarcely knew, a sculptor named Auguste Clésinger. Solange, unlike Maurice, shared Chopin's aristocratic leanings, and Clésinger had led her to believe he would provide her with wealth and an elevated position in society. But she soon discovered that her husband had lied about his means and his prospects; he was not only penniless but heavily in debt. Her disillusionment so embittered her that she willfully took revenge upon the young cousin George had adopted, spreading spiteful lies about Augustine and causing a suitor who loved Augustine to break off their engagement. When George upbraided Solange for her cruel behavior, the troublemaking young woman went straight to Chopin in Paris. She deftly persuaded him of her own innocence in the matter and tried to turn him against her mother. She insinuated that George was carrying on love affairs with other men in Chopin's absence. Such tales were pure

invention but, morbidly jealous, Chopin chose to believe them. He wrote George a strained letter, she
wrote back to him coolly, and then their correspondence broke off. Though George asked after Chopin
frequently, the scant news she received of him came
only through mutual friends.

So it was that when the disease which had been stead-
ily destroying the composer took his life—in October of
1849—George was not at his deathbed. He had been
away giving concerts in England for much of the time,
and the two had never reconciled. They had seen each
other only once, by chance on a stairway in Paris for a
mere passing moment. . . .

> I took his hand. It was as cold as ice and it was trembling.
> I wanted to talk to him but he hastened away. It was my
> turn to say he loved me no longer but I spared him that
> pain. I was never to see him again. . . . People said that
> he asked after me, missed me, loved me devotedly till
> the end. They thought it right to hide this from me till
> that moment. They thought it right to hide from him too
> that I was ever ready to rush to his side. They did well,
> if the emotion of seeing me would have shortened his
> life by one day or even by a single hour.

A few years later, in her memoirs, George tried with
those words to console herself for a death which
"affected me profoundly." But in the summer of 1847,
after Chopin's departure from Nohant, she had no notion that the piano in the downstairs parlor would never
respond again to the touch of his "velvet fingers." During that summer serious financial problems took up
most of her thoughts.

It was becoming increasingly clear that Solange's

irresponsible husband would never properly provide for his wife, and George longed to find some way of securing her daughter's welfare. But writing on behalf of a republic, which seemed more than ever only a dream for the distant future, had thoroughly drained her health and her pocketbook. The sales of her novels had fallen off drastically. Moreover, she no longer felt physically capable of writing at her old tempo, and when she made up her accounts in the fall of 1847, she discovered that she was 30,000 francs in debt.

A friend suggested she put fiction aside for the moment and write her memoirs. It seemed a possible solution. George signed a contract with the publisher Ernest Dupuy to provide five volumes, for which she would be paid a total of 130,000 francs. It was a considerable sum, enough to furnish an income for Solange and a dowry for Augustine and to pay off her own debts. She immediately set to work and, by January of 1848, was deeply involved in the new project.

Indeed, she became so absorbed by it that she was only dimly aware of what was happening in the world around her. When Maurice, whom she had sent to Paris to fetch material on her great-grandfather, the Count de Saxe, did not return for several weeks, she was puzzled. She wrote him to come back immediately, but there was no reply. Then she learned the reason—with the same stunned surprise with which the entire country received the news. The population of Paris had suddenly risen up in arms—overthrown the monarchy, burned the royal throne and set up the provisional government of a republic! George put pen aside and has-

tened to the capital to witness the unexpected fulfill-
ment of a dream.

9

George found her son installed in a little attic room
overlooking Paris's Odéon theater and the Luxembourg Gardens beyond. The streets of the capital,
though calm now, still lay in disorder. During the recent
uprising, thousands of trees had been pulled down and
turned into barricades by insurgent workers, artisans,
students. . . . Maurice, an ardent republican like his
mother, had been among them. From his excited eye-
witness account and from what she had learned before
leaving Nohant, George was able to reconstruct the
events which had led up to the social drama of 1848.
  For some time the entire population of France, with
the exception of powerful banking interests, had been
harboring grievances against the monarchy. Poverty
among the peasants, who had suffered from a potato
blight which destroyed their crops, had intensified with
rising prices. Workers' salaries had been cut by more
than half, and unemployment had reached vast proportions. The growing industrial bourgeoisie, who owned
the factories, had been discontented because it had no
real voice in the government; the right to vote, paid for
by an excessive annual fee, belonged largely to ultra-
rich bankers. Early in February, the bourgeoisie had
called for a demonstration on the Champs-Elysées for

electoral reforms which would extend the vote. The government had forbidden the demonstration, but the people had taken to the streets anyway, crying "Long live the Reform!" Fifty of the demonstrators had been shot down by a regiment of the king's riflemen.

After that, events had moved quickly. Parisians had taken up arms and, from the tops of hastily constructed barricades, they had called for the overthrow of the monarchy. Though the National Guard was sent out to quell the insurrection, it refused to fire on the populace. Then King Louis-Philippe, taking fright, abdicated. A provisional government of the Second Republic was set up in the City Hall with the poet Alphonse de Lamartine as Foreign Minister, the lawyer Alexandre Ledru-Rollin as Minister of the Interior, the socialist Louis Blanc as Minister of Labor. . . .

George went to call on the government, leading a delegation of republican friends from Berry. She hoped to obtain appointments for them in the provinces where formerly arch-conservatives had held sway. Her name had become a password in republican circles and she was swept through crowded corridors and packed anterooms directly into the offices of the Minister of the Interior, Ledru-Rollin. The Minister, who admired George, agreed to support the candidates she proposed.

Though the government had taken power only temporarily, pending general elections, George was pleased to find it already running the country along republican lines. The vote was granted to all male citizens over twenty-one. The "right to employment" was recognized and national workshops were set up for the jobless. The vision George shared with Liszt of "culture for the people" was becoming a reality as the Comédie Française changed its name to the Théâtre de la République and cut the prices of its seats so that the poor could watch classical drama being performed by the finest actors and actresses of France. The gaping holes along the boulevards were being filled in and green "liberty trees" were sprouting up all over the city.

The government needed writers to disseminate its republican ideas before the forthcoming elections, and Ledru-Rollin asked George for her help. She rented a large, third-floor room on the rue de Condé and set to work. There she turned out articles for a new republican weekly and began to write the *Bulletins de la République*. These bulletins, issued by the Ministry of the Interior, were the voice which the government used for speaking to the French people. Thus George acted as the new republic's unofficial Minister of Propaganda, a unique and unheard-of role for a woman.

Maurice had been appointed Mayor of Nohant, and in March George wrote her son from Paris: "Here I am doing a statesman's work. I made out two government circulars today, one for the Ministry of Public Education and one for the Ministry of the Interior. It amuses me to think that this material will go out addressed to 'all mayors' and that you will be getting instructions through official channels from your *mother*. People are after me on all sides and I don't know which way to turn." She was forty-three, and yet, "My heart is full, my brain on fire," she wrote. "I've forgotten all my physical aches, all my personal griefs. I'm alive, strong, active."

Parisians fighting on the barricades in 1848.

A caricature of George Sand
carrying the portfolio of the
Minister of the Interior,
Ledru-Rollin.

Through her writing on behalf of the republican cause, George soon became known as the "Muse of the Republic." She was so prominent in political circles that before long a campaign was launched to see her elected to the new National Assembly. But though her name was entered on forty different lists of candidates, George opposed the campaign on principle. Women, to her mind, should play no deciding role in politics until they had first of all won their civil rights. Only as educated, free agents, liberated from the legal and intellectual domination of men, she held, would they be able to participate in public activities intelligently. Moreover, she did not believe that equal rights would be granted women under a government controlled by industrialists any more than they had been granted under kings. Only a socialist republic, she felt, could place women and men on the same footing.

George was more preoccupied now than ever with the idea of socialism, which for decades had been discussed in the radical salons she frequented and in secret societies formed by workers. At first it had been considered a utopian dream. In February of this same year of 1848, however, it took on new significance when a twenty-nine-year-old German philosopher, Karl Marx, published the *Communist Manifesto.* In this document, put out by the Communist League organized in London the year before, Marx expounded the theory that socialism was the inevitable next step in the historical development of human society. He called upon workers in every country to overthrow their ruling classes and set up classless societies in which the wealth of the country, both factory and farm, would be run by and belong to all the people.

George had always felt closer to the commoners from whose ranks she had sprung on her mother's side than to the aristocrats on her father's side. She identified herself now with the socialist ideal. She did not believe, along with Karl Marx, that a violent struggle was inevitable; she felt that the ruling class could be persuaded to give way peacefully to the will of the progressive masses. Still, she staunchly declared herself a socialist. Not all republicans agreed with her, however, as she pointed out in the diary she kept during the turbulent spring months of 1848:

> On the morrow of the February revolution, everyone called himself a republican. Still, it was easy to see from the outset that profound disagreement separated them into two distinct camps—into the republicans of *yesterday* and those of *tomorrow* . . . into republicans who were purely and simply politicians, to whom the routed monarchists had rallied, and socialist republicans made up by and large of the workers of Paris. The day before yesterday, the lines of demarcation were blurred; today, an abyss divides them.

George felt that a clash of arms could be avoided if the provisional government stood firmly behind sound republican principles. But already Lamartine, head of the provisional government, was wavering. Delegates from the countryside had brought back reports that the peasants in the provinces were lagging far behind Parisian workers in their revolutionary zeal. Since three-fourths of the peasants were illiterate and without political education, they would most probably vote conservative local politicians into office in the coming elections. Unnerved by these reports and anxious over their own political futures, government ministers began to beat a retreat. They sabotaged the progressive social measures they themselves had initiated. When bankers refused to finance the national workshops for the unemployed, the Minister of Public Works levied a burdensome tax on the poor. As a result of such measures, the "abyss" widened ominously. Tension mounted in the capital as working people, who had placed their faith in the provisional government, began to feel that it was betraying them.

Through her influence on Lamartine and Ledru-Rollin, George tried to prevent this "betrayal." She urged the government to make an effort to educate the backward peasants rather than give way to conservative pressure. She suggested that delegations of workers be sent to all parts of France to explain to the peasants that their true interests lay with the republican cause. She drafted a proposal for a more democratic electoral law, too, that would establish a vote by popular majority. She pursued government ministers from office to office, sought to put new heart into the vacillating Lamartine, to strengthen the flagging zeal of others. She also tried to impart courage to her own son, who was complaining despairingly of the antagonistic behavior of the reactionaries in his district.

"Don't be upset by threats," she wrote him. "Every revolutionary these days, whether he is a member of the provisional government or Mayor of Nohant, must expect to meet with resistance, reaction, hostility. Can it be otherwise? What merit would there be in calling oneself a revolutionary if everything happened by itself and if one had only to want something in order to achieve it? No, for people like us, life is and perhaps always will be a continuous struggle. Has mine been anything else since the day I was born?"

Not many government ministers in Paris were fired by the same determination. Their sympathies lay basically with the industrialists, and they were more terrified of the socialist-minded working class than they were of the conservative peasants. They studied the proposals George submitted and passed them around diligently from office to office, but ultimately they forgot them.

Meanwhile, George saw precious time being lost. She foresaw the danger of an unenlightened electorate undermining, even destroying, the republican victory she held dear. If this came to pass, she was willing to abandon her belief in peaceful solutions, for then there would be only one way to save the republic—throw up new barricades and wage a new armed struggle which would place a genuinely republican government in power. She said as much in what became the famous *Bulletin No. 16*, issued officially by the Ministry of the Interior but written, as most people knew, by George Sand. After *Bulletin No. 16* appeared, containing words which were tantamount to a call to the barricades, many moderates held George responsible for the clashes which took place following the elections in April.

On the eve of these elections, however, the warring political factions in the capital momentarily forgot their quarrels as they joined to celebrate a Holiday of Brotherhood. For twelve hours George participated in a "gigantic and sublime human spectacle." A parade, led by the republican army in full dress uniform, set off from the Bastille and the Observatory across the city toward the Arch of Triumph and beyond, forming a line of march several miles long. Mingling in the army's glittering ranks, as George wrote, were "the ragged and sacred rabble, men and women of every age, singing, shouting and applauding . . . one million human souls, who forgot all bitterness and forgave the past as they embraced each other from one end of Paris to the other, raising the cry *Long Live Human Brotherhood!*" The impressive display of mass solidarity put new heart into republican militants.

To these same militants, however, the elections on April twenty-third came as a severe disappointment. As had been feared, the provinces outvoted the capital and the majority of deputies elected to the National Assembly turned out to be moderates and monarchists. But the republic was still in existence, and George refused to regard the future with the despair that had overtaken the liberal Ledru-Rollin and placed him in the same camp with the increasingly conservative Lamartine. She continued to argue with both men; one contemporary observed her stretched out on the lawn of the Chamber of Deputies, talking with Ledru-Rollin and Lamartine while a sentry stood guard so that no one would disturb their discussion.

During this troubled period, while the moderate government tried to control the discontented populace in the capital, George was invited to a luncheon given by a visiting British member of Parliament. The historian Alexis de Tocqueville, well known for his writings on the young United States of America, was present. As a wary liberal, he considered the socialist George Sand in the "enemy's camp," yet he was impressed by this celebrated Muse of the Republic.

"It was the first time I had had direct contact with someone who could and would tell me what was going on in the opposite camp," he wrote. "Madame Sand painted a remarkably vivid picture of how the Parisian workers lived, what their numbers were, how they were organized and armed. She talked of their intentions, thoughts, passions and fierce determination. I considered the picture overdrawn, but it was not at all, as the future proved."

George was concerned for the fate of the conservatives in the event of a popular victory. "Try to convince your friends," she told Tocqueville, "not to push the people to the breaking point and drive them into the streets, and I shall try to instill patience in those on my side. For, believe me, if there is a battle, all of your kind will perish in it."

The discontented working people in the capital, however, were no longer willing to listen to those who preached "patience." On May fifteenth Parisian crowds marched on the National Assembly, declared it dissolved, and proclaimed a socialist republic. But the army cleared the Assembly with bayonets and arrested the revolutionary leaders.

George herself was threatened with arrest and was advised to flee the country. Instead she went back to Nohant, where she continued to write political articles. She no longer wrote for the government, however, but contributed to a socialist opposition paper, *La Vraie République* (The True Republic). In fact, she redoubled her efforts on behalf of that "true republic," for she felt it was not yet lost. In this year of 1848, proletarian revolutions were spreading throughout Europe. There were workers' insurrections in Austria, Germany, Hungary, Italy, Poland. . . . It seemed increasingly clear to her that the May fifteenth attempt on the National Assembly was only a prelude to a new uprising in Paris which would decide the future of France.

During these desperate days, some of George's friends fretted because she was neglecting her own literary work. To one friend, who had written her about "poetry, inspiration, glory and genius," she answered: "You are speaking a language which I no longer understand. To cultivate one's talent is well and good in calm periods, in restful, melancholy waiting periods. But when humanity fights, suffers, bleeds, I can't think about my muse and my lyre. I am not one of these self-indulgent intellectuals who keeps feeling his pulse to see if inspiration still flows in his veins. I don't see how one can coddle one's personality when a universe is fighting for its life or its death."

In June the government closed down the national workshops for the unemployed, and the army was granted dictatorial powers. The working people rose in rebellion. Overnight they threw up some four hundred barricades in the streets of the capital and the surrounding suburbs. Railwaymen, carpenters, mechanics —men of all trades—took up arms. Those who could find no other weapon grabbed hammers or shovels. Women and children helped melt down cannonballs, dress the wounded and bring water and food to the insurgents.

On June twenty-fourth, the people of Paris charged the City Hall, attacking it on four sides, and came within sixty paces of seizing the seat of the government. But the Minister of War, General Eugène Cavaignac, who was known for his brutal massacres in Algeria, arrived at the head of the regular army supported by 24,000 members of the mobile guard. During the bitter battle which lasted several days, hundreds of working people were killed. Even when the last insurgent barricade had been forced to surrender and General Cavaignac had arrested 25,000 men and condemned 3,500 to deportation, his troops pursued the populace through the streets. They shot down any man who wore a worker's smock or had traces of gunpowder on his face, and left 2,000 more to die lying on the bloodstained cobblestones of the capital.

In Nohant, George was appalled by reports of the carnage. "I have ceased to believe in a republic which begins by killing its proletarians," she wrote. "Today I am ashamed of being a Frenchwoman, when only yesterday I was proud to call myself one." There were daily threats to burn down her home. When she walked through the streets of the village, people shouted after her "Down with communists!" But, though all her friends had left the countryside, George refused to be cowed by the "small storms" which blew up around her. She was much more concerned about the fate of the French populace with whom she had, as she had told Tocqueville, thrown in her lot.

The radical press was closed down by the government, the socialist party was suppressed, "liberty trees" were felled and, later, freedom of assembly was abolished. In September of 1848, the one-time liberal Louis Bonaparte—nephew of the late Emperor Napoleon I—was elected to the legislature. That December he became Prince-President. During the next few years he consolidated his power through conspiratorial political maneuvers until in 1851 he staged a coup d'état and dissolved the legislature. He then launched an autocratic reign of terror in the country involving wholesale arrests, deportations and executions of men who held republican convictions.

Once again people urged George to flee the country. The republic, she knew, was lost. Her romantic dream of the rich voluntarily abandoning power to share and share alike with the poor in the spirit of human brotherhood was shattered. But her revolutionary friends were in danger. Every day there were new arrests. Many of these revolutionaries had seen in the new kind of war that had come into being in 1848—a war not between nations but between opposing classes within a nation—a means of achieving a socialist republic. Though an ardent socialist herself, George did not agree with them totally. She recoiled from the violence class war now seemed to make inevitable. Yet she felt she could not turn her back on her friends. She wrote a letter requesting an audience with Louis Napoleon.

The fact that George was a cousin on her father's side to the royal family stood her in good stead. The police granted her the right of "free passage" to the capital and, on January 30, 1852, she entered the Elysée Palace and confronted the head of the French government. The Prince-President received George not only with deference but with warmth, for he had known and ad-

Manuscript fragment of George Sand's preface to the French edition of Harriet Beecher Stowe's novel *Uncle Tom's Cabin*.

10

In October of 1854, the first chapters of George's memoirs began to appear in *La Presse:*

> My mother rarely spoke about her parents because she hardly knew them, having lost them when she was still a child. Who was her paternal grandfather? She had no idea, nor do I. And her grandmother? Not a whit more is known of her. So it is that the genealogy of the common people cannot compete with that of the rich and powerful of this earth. No title, no coat of arms, no painting preserves the memory of those obscure generations who pass through this world without leaving a trace. The poor man's death is total; his grave is sealed by the scorn of the rich who stride over it without even knowing it is human dust they disturb with a disdainful foot. . . .

During the financial recession that had followed the 1848 revolution, she had been forced to lay her work on these memoirs aside because her publisher had been unable to pay her. Burdened with debts, she had turned to popular fiction to write two pastoral novels. In *La Petite Fadette* (*Little Fadette*), and *François le Champi* (*The Country Waif*), she had treated her peasant characters, if sometimes sentimentally, with a dignity and understanding rare in contemporary fiction. They had instantly won back for George the readership she had lost in previous years. Soon after, she signed a contract with *La Presse* and now she was busy producing volume after volume of what was turning into a monumental work entitled *Histoire de ma vie* (*The History of My Life*).

George had no desire to expose the intimate details of her personal life, nor did she wish to take revenge upon her enemies. "Let not the people who have done me evil be frightened, I have forgotten them; let no lover of scandal rejoice, I am not writing for him." Instead she was presenting, in what is now generally agreed to be one of her finest creations, a medley of biography and of social and political ideas, along with her view of the eventful century in which she lived. But though George was fascinated by this work growing under her hands, it was not her only project.

The actor Pierre Bocage had paid a visit to Nohant and persuaded her to adapt *François le Champi* for the stage. Its production in Paris proved a success and now she was writing other plays as well. As she turned more and more to the theater, she saw ten of her plays produced in the capital over the next decade. Some met with an indifferent reception but others enjoyed packed houses month after month. In three of them, the leading roles were played by the great Sarah Bernhardt.

Maurice had created an ingenious puppet theater at Nohant which offered a rare opportunity for amusement during these first politically grim years under the Empire. Before the little stage Maurice had constructed, George sat enthralled as oil lamps and reflectors were trained in shifting colors on the painted and expressive faces of little figures her son had carved out of linden wood. He made them perform in clever sketches of his own improvisation. Later George wrote

L'Homme de neige (*The Snow Man*), a novel inspired by her son's puppet theater.

There was also a full-sized theater at Nohant where fortnightly performances were given. George had ordered it built in what had formerly been the billiard room on the ground floor. It could seat fifty people, and she used it as a testing ground for her dramatic works in progress. She herself acted in these tryouts, as did all the members of the household and their guests. Maurice painted the scenery, George sewed the costumes, and it was rarely hard to find a full cast, for Nohant was usually filled with Maurice's friends. There were the painter Eugène Lambert, who specialized in wildlife drawings, the lawyer Émile Aucante, the republican journalist Victor Borie, and many others. Arriving in relays, they turned into more or less permanent residents, and George enjoyed the youthful high spirits they brought to her quiet country retreat.

Among these houseguests at Nohant was a talented engraver, Alexandre Manceau. He was lean and frail, with a quick intelligence in his fine gray eyes. George was pleased to call him a "proletarian," for he was the son of a caretaker at the Luxembourg Palace. He was younger than she and his health was fragile, but he possessed a solidity of character plus a calm, disciplined attitude toward work which made him someone upon whom she could lean. He became her private secretary and later he took charge of her professional dealings with publishers and theater directors. His loyalty and understanding, and the moral support he offered, made Manceau the indispensable partner in George's life for many years.

The study of nature had fascinated George ever since childhood. She had communicated this fascination to her son and his friends, and they spent afternoons tramping with her over the countryside near Nohant. They searched out the four species of heather which George fed to her caterpillars. They combed the ground for rare and interesting stones, each person equipped with a small geological hammer.

In the evenings everyone gathered around a large, oval table which the village carpenter had built for her grandmother when George was four years old. The soft light from a delicately tinted Venetian chandelier shed its rays on George's graying head as she worked correcting proofs of her memoirs or stitching a costume for one of Maurice's puppets. The others mounted specimens, or sketched, or wrote comic verses or played chess. More often than not someone read aloud . . . a novel of Balzac's, or Sir Walter Scott's *Ivanhoe*, or poems by Victor Hugo which the author had sent to George.

At midnight George always rose to retire to her study. There Manceau had prepared her oil lamp, laid out paper, pens, ink, Turkish tobacco, and a glass of sugared water. She wrote until dawn, turning out her disciplined quota of twenty pages. In the mornings, while "Madame" slept, the guests were thrown upon their own resources, but all their needs were looked after by an efficient staff of servants. A small box was provided for requests; one had only to write it on a slip of paper indicating one's room number to discover what one had asked for, at six o'clock the next morning, outside one's door.

The salon at Nohant, where George Sand's family and friends gathered in the evenings around the old oval table.

Solange visited infrequently. Her taste for excitement, which she could not satisfy at "boring" Nohant, often made her more of a trial than a pleasure. It was said that even the cocks crowed more belligerently when she was there. The young woman had inherited her mother's rebellious spirit but had never found a productive outlet for it. She was constantly quarreling with her husband and it was usually during a marital rift that Solange put in her unexpected appearances. George minded less than the others, for Solange sometimes brought along her little girl, Nini, whom George adored. She spent long hours with her granddaughter, building little fairyland grottoes for her in the garden, walking with her in the woods, teaching her to read. When Solange and her husband, who led spendthrift and irregular lives, at last decided upon a legal separation, the courts awarded George custody of her precious Nini. The child's father appealed the ruling and Nini was kept at boarding school while the court decision was pending. When he took her for an outing one cold day in nothing but a light summer dress, she fell ill, contracted a fever and, in a matter of days, died.

George was so griefstricken at the loss of her grandchild that Manceau and Maurice sought some means to distract her. In the spring of 1855 they decided to take her to Italy. Manceau dipped into his savings to pay for the journey, which lasted almost seven months as they traveled to Genoa, Pisa, Florence. In the Papal city of Rome, George felt so oppressed by the presence and power of the clergy that she, who had once wanted to become a nun, wrote two anticlerical novels, *La Daniella* and *Mademoiselle La Quintinie*. These works earned her the disapproval of the imperial censors but gave her a new following among students who idolized her as a champion of their liberal views.

After the Italian journey, back at Nohant, her life began to be interrupted increasingly by people seeking help from the celebrated Madame Sand, known for her generosity as well as her influential connections at court. Wives of imprisoned republicans came to beg her to intercede on their husbands' behalves with the Emperor's cousin, the more liberal Prince Jérôme Bonaparte, who was George's friend. Destitute writers came seeking aid in publishing their works. Or some farmer in Nohant, whose crops had done badly, knocked at her gate to ask for help for his family. She assisted them whenever she could . . . so much so that she became known as "The Good Lady of Nohant." But, ever pressured by work, she longed at times to flee to some quieter spot.

In the little village of Gargilesse in the hilly region of Berry, Manceau came upon a small house which he bought and fitted out for George. In this isolated area where cliffs plunged to the blue river Creuse and the protected valley gloried in a rich and almost tropical greenery, she discovered the solitude for which she longed. Whenever obligations at Nohant overpowered her, she would disappear to Gargilesse with Manceau. Over the years she worked on thirteen novels there.

She visited Paris only when her presence was required at rehearsals of her new plays or when there was some outstanding play being staged which she did not want to miss. During an intermission of *La Dame aux camélias* (*Camille*) by Alexandre Dumas the younger,

George met its author for the first time. Famous in his own right, he was the illegitimate son of the celebrated writer of *The Three Musketeers,* Alexandre Dumas the elder. The elder Dumas had known and admired George for many years, considering her one of the "great ones" of the century. But it was between her and the younger Dumas that a strong friendship developed.

Like Sophie Dupin, the mother of the younger Dumas had been a poor seamstress. His sufferings at the hands of schoolmates, who had taunted him over his illegitimacy, had helped him to develop the defensive shell of a cynic and a pessimist. He had a biting wit and thought little of women, considering them limited creatures deserving of their "slavish condition." Despite this, however, Dumas became deeply devoted to George, for somewhere beneath the pessimist in him lay an idealist.

Dumas often visited Nohant, drawn by the energy, the strength of will and the gentle understanding of a woman whose equal, he told her once, had never been born. As he and George walked along the wooded paths or swam together in the river, he opened his usually guarded heart to her about his problems with his work, or with some woman he loved, or with his difficult-to-handle genius of a father. She always helped him.

"When I was your age, I was just as tormented as you," she told him, "and much sicker in soul and body. I grew weary of digging down into myself and others, and a day came when I said: 'To the Devil with all that!' I am an optimist in spite of everything that has torn me apart; it is probably my only good quality. You'll see, it'll come to you, too." But the relationship was not one-sided, for Dumas offered her his generous professional advice and help in the writing of her plays.

In 1864 *Le Marquis de Villemer*, a play she based on one of her own novels, was scheduled to open in Paris at the Odéon theater. There were rumors that organized religious groups were planning a demonstration against its anticlerical author. Parisian students came out by the thousands on opening night to support George. They filled the cobblestoned square before the theater, crying "Long live George Sand!" Those who had come to hoot at the play were overwhelmed by the cheering and shouting, as well as by the presence in the theater of the imperial family. At the end of the performance, there was tumultuous applause. Hundreds of people came up to George in the foyer to shake her hand and to kiss her. Outside, so dense were the enthusiastic crowds pushing toward the entrance that Napoleon III was obliged to make his way on foot toward his waiting carriage, which had been unable to drive up to the theater steps.

George, in her sixtieth year, enjoyed one of the most spectacular successes of her long career. The major critics of Paris heaped praises upon her play. French youth called her the "Great Woman of the Opposition." She was the first woman permitted to attend the dinners at Magny's—a Left Bank restaurant where the elite of Paris intellectuals held fortnightly gatherings. Even the antifeminist Goncourt brothers welcomed her there. Authors of the *Journal des Goncourt* which commented on Paris life over a period of forty years, they described the "chiseled delicacy" of George's features at this time and "her good face, soft and serene, the

Alexandre Manceau. Portrait by Auguste Lehmann.

colors faded but the outlines still finely drawn in pale, amber tints."

She no longer donned a man's disguise in public. Sometimes she wore a plain grayish brown silk dress with sturdy walking shoes, sometimes a gay peach-colored print and at times, even now, a flashing red petticoat. Marie d'Agoult, from whom Liszt had long since parted, disapproved: "What I cannot forgive in someone of her breeding," she said, "is her lack of propriety, the shocking way she dresses, the clowning about she encourages at Nohant, her bohemian, art-student behavior. In a woman of her age, it's inexcusable."

George paid little attention. The one person whose criticism troubled her was her son's. Maurice was married now and the father of a son of his own by his Italian bride, Lina Calamatta. But Manceau had taken quiet command of most affairs at Nohant and Maurice had grown resentful of his presence in the house. One day Maurice forced Manceau into a quarrel and then delivered an ultimatum to his mother—she must choose between the two. George stood by her son, then passed the night in tears as she tried to imagine herself separated from Manceau, who had cared for her devotedly for well over a decade. In the morning, she changed her mind; if Maurice wished to be uncontested master at Nohant, then she would leave the estate to him and go off with Manceau. It was arranged amicably enough despite the underlying tension, and George and Manceau went to live in a little house in the suburbs of Paris.

Before she left Nohant, Maurice and Lina tried preaching "abstinence" to George, who, it seemed to them, was as reckless with her vitality and her heart as if she were still a young woman. George listened to their lecture without raising any objections, for she loved them both deeply. But that night in her diary she wrote:

> Abstinence! Abstinence from what, you young imbeciles? Abstain all your lives, if you can, from doing harm to others. But did God create what is good so that we should deprive ourselves of it? Should we abstain from enjoying the sun's warmth and the fragrance of lilacs in flower? As for me, I work hard . . . without abstaining from the regret that I do not work still harder.

No sooner had she and Manceau installed themselves in their new house, however, than Maurice sent for his mother again. He had taken his wife and child to his father's home in Gascony, and there his little son, Marc-Antoine, had fallen desperately ill with dysentery. George hastened to Gascony, but arrived too late—the child had died that morning. Her grief was heavy—she had lost yet another grandchild—but still she tried to console her stricken son and daughter-in-law. This was one of the rare occasions since their separation that she came face to face with Casimir. Both were in mourning, but nevertheless they had little to say to each other. Casimir was living with his housekeeper, by whom he had had an illegitimate child. When George left she gave her hand to her husband for the last time. He died, in 1871, without their meeting again.

Back at home, George grew concerned over Manceau's health. Like Chopin, he had begun spitting blood; consumption, she realized, was running its tragic course. Throughout their years together Manceau had carefully noted down daily events in a diary he shared with George. When he became bedridden and too weak to write, George took over the entries. She hid the gravity of his condition from him by writing in their joint diary that the treatment the doctors were administering would surely lead to his recovery. Meanwhile, she rarely left the side of the doomed man.

Manceau died in August of 1865. George felt "utterly broken" by her loss, yet she wrote her son: "I shan't be ill. Do not worry. I refuse to fall ill. . . ." Maurice came to fetch her back to Nohant. Now that Manceau was gone, he was eager for his mother to make it her home again. Lina was pregnant and soon she gave birth to a little girl who turned out to have the same dark, velvety eyes George had inherited from her father and Maurice from her. She was christened Aurore.

George was in her mid-sixties now and had lost many of those who had been close to her in her youth. Her half brother Hippolyte had died in 1848, Balzac two years later, while the year 1869 took away Sainte-Beuve. Among the friends left to her, perhaps the most important was Gustave Flaubert. At the Magny dinners, George discovered in the novelist—a balding bachelor, with a drooping blond mustache and a powerful build—the only man present with whom she really felt at ease. Unlike George, the author of *Madame Bovary* scoffed at the concept of social progress, disdained "novels with a purpose" and often spent entire nights tormentedly searching for the one precise and perfect word. At the same time he shared with George a revulsion for the acquisitive society which was flourishing under Napoleon III. He claimed, too, that in order to be truly human a person must "vibrate" to the limits of his capacity regardless of the pain or pleasure involved. In this their two fundamentally fearless natures were in accord.

Shy of his fellow creatures and highly nervous, Flaubert chose to live a secluded life with his aging mother in the village of Croisset in Normandy. He invited George to visit him there. In his comfortable, well-appointed house he gave her a cozy room under the eaves where she could work during the day. In the evenings they dined with his mother and the charming old lady's friends; then Flaubert invariably took George to his library where he read to her from one of his manuscripts. Afterward they talked . . . once until half past two in the morning. They grew hungry and went downstairs to raid the kitchen for a bit of cold chicken, took a turn in the garden to draw fresh water from the pump, then went back upstairs again where they smoked and talked until almost dawn.

After George's departure, Flaubert wrote to her. "Everyone here treasures you. Under what star were you born that you possess such a quantity of rare qualities? We do get on well together, don't we?"

George urged Flaubert to come to Nohant, but he usually refused her invitations, clinging to his own hidden corner of the world. George understood his idiosyncracies. As she wrote him, "You do not have an itching foot as I have, always ready to be on the move. You live in your dressing gown—that archenemy of freedom and the active life."

She kept up a steady correspondence with Flaubert while pursuing her own "active life"; she found she was beginning to see better without than with her glasses,

Gustave Flaubert. Photograph by Mulnier.

and she could still run up the stairs at Nohant as briskly as her dogs. Their letters were in a way an extension of their nightly discussions or, rather, friendly arguments, in Normandy. They disagreed about art, religion, politics, yet when all was said and done they were, as George wrote, just "two old troubadours, who believe in love, in art and in ideals and who go on singing while everyone around us hoots and jabbers."

But if Flaubert and Dumas admired George, there were others who did not. Charles Baudelaire, author of *Les Fleurs du mal* (*Flowers of Evil*) and a poet with an anguished soul, was thoroughly maddened by the cheerful moralist in George. He found her writings wordy and unutterably stupid. "The things she has said about her mother," he wrote, "the things she says about poetry . . . her love for the working class . . . ! That some people can become dewy eyed over such a latrine is proof enough of the depths to which men in this century have sunk."

That Baudelaire could write this in the last half of the nineteenth century was also perhaps "proof enough" that the Romantic school had died out. It had become the fashion now to make fun of the *mal du siècle*—the "sickness" of that bygone era when the individual focused attention almost exclusively on private sensations, whether of grief or of ecstacy. Though George was identified with this Romantic school, she had separated herself from it in many ways. Once she had considered the heart the sole reliable guide to a human being's acts. Now reason, intellect, the critical approach of the scientist counted more for her.

She did not repudiate the Romantics' contribution in

197

defying narrow conventions that had blocked artistic and social progress. "Maybe our sickness had more good in it than the reaction which followed it," she wrote, "than this thirst for money, for pleasures uninspired by an ideal, for ambition without limit. They don't seem to me to picture very nobly the 'health' of the century." But she had nevertheless left purely emotional Romanticism far behind. "Do not tell me that studying the laws of nature and searching for the basic causes of things dries up the heart or slows the flight of the imagination," she wrote. The skeptic of the tormented days of *Lélia* refused to become a skeptic again simply because an ideal human society had not yet been realized on earth.

"A new *I* is beginning . . ." George had written. In the twilight of her days, this new *I* emerged. Throughout her whole life, however, George continued to develop and to gain new followers. For many years she had been considered the great woman of the century in France, but she was also a celebrity throughout the world. When her admirers abroad visited Paris they sought her out; among these were the ardent American feminist Margaret Fuller. Mary Ann Evans, the English novelist who wrote under the pseudonym George Eliot, said of George Sand, "I cannot read six pages of hers without feeling that it is given to her to delineate human passion and its results with such truthfulness, such nicety of discrimination, such tragic power and withal such loving gentle humour that one might live a century with nothing but one's own dull faculties and not know so much as those six pages will suggest." She was widely read in Russia too; Fëdor Dostoevsky thought that "the vigor of her mind and of her talent was almost unique." In the United States her novels on working-class life influenced Walt Whitman's belief that a poet must have a social mission, reinforced his faith in democracy and is even said to have affected the way he dressed; in his portrait that appeared in *Leaves of Grass* he abandoned frock coat and silk hat for worker's clothes.

In her upstairs study at Nohant, bound volumes of George's novels, plays and memoirs stood in impressive rows now upon the shelves. But for the most part George thought little of her own writings. When she saw the agonies Flaubert suffered, she felt depressed; by comparison, she wrote him, her work seemed unpolished, slipshod. "In your books," Flaubert answered, "ideas flow like a river, wide and unceasing. In mine they are a mere trickle. It takes an enormous artistic effort for me to produce a waterfall."

But the secret of the novel, George believed, was in communicating its theme subtly without the reader's being consciously aware of it. She claimed she had never been able to achieve such a marriage of form and content. "I just plow on straight ahead of me, stupid as a cabbage and patient as a Berrichon peasant," she wrote to Flaubert. "Now and then the retired old troubadour sings a little serenade to the moon, not caring much whether he sings it well or off key as long as he can pour out the melodies which keep on running in his head."

The melodies still ran on and, as she approached her seventies, George kept on writing. Meanwhile, she drew increasing enjoyment from her simple occupations at

George Sand at sixty. Photograph by Nadar.

Nohant. She went swimming in the tree-shaded river; she gave lessons to little Aurore. She even found time to instruct a trumpeter in the village fire brigade to play a flourish. She herself learned Reveille, Parade, Action, Dismiss, Assembly; and, as she wrote a friend, "Now I can bugle away with the best of them!"

As always, there were frequent visitors. These days it was Flaubert, Dumas, and the great Russian novelist Ivan Turgenev who gathered around the long, oval table of an evening while George played Gluck or Mozart on the piano, or they read aloud to one another from their latest works or joined in the lively puppet shows.

In 1870 George's corner of Berry was cut off from the capital by the Franco-Prussian War. France was defeated by Germany and an armistice was signed. Then there was revolution—and the socialist Commune—and then a bloody counterrevolution and another bourgeois republic. But the countryside was relatively untouched by these upheavals in the capital and afterward life at Nohant went on in its habitual rhythm. There was a new granddaughter now, Titite, but little Aurore, with her passion for learning and her need to "race forward at a gallop," remained George's favorite. She loved telling stories to the child and published some of them in one of her last books, *Contes d'une grand-mère* (*Tales of a Grandmother*). George was ending her life as she had begun it, making up fairy tales . . . for another child with the same dark, velvety eyes as the little girl who had stood long ago between four cane-bottomed chairs in a Paris garret.

In the early spring of 1876, George was seventy-one.

Healthy and strong, she was convinced she would live for many years to come. But in May, an intestinal obstruction forced her to bed. Her condition became critical. Well-meaning but bungling doctors tried vainly to save her. After many days of pain, George called her children and grandchildren around her and tenderly, almost absently, bade them farewell. She murmured a last, unintelligible phrase, "Leave the greenness. . . ." The others guessed what she meant: she wished to be buried in the tiny graveyard at Nohant, beside her father and her grandmother, beneath the common grass.

It was June 8, 1876, and George Sand was dead. But she was to die as well a second death. As the years went by, her works came to be ignored for the most part. Her personality was deliberately misrepresented, and later generations too often had an image of her merely as a loose, cigar-smoking caricature of her real self. There were two reasons for this second death. She was a radical in politics; and she was a woman. But, as time passed, history gradually caught up with her. Others joined in the pursuit of goals she cherished. Her works have begun to appear in new editions. Young people have begun to draw inspiration once more from the daring woman around whom Parisian students once crowded shouting "Long Live George Sand!" And her name has come to recapture some of the influence that it bore that gray June morning in 1876 when close friends traveled to Nohant for her funeral.

Dumas was there. So was Flaubert, who wept inconsolably. Peasants from Nohant, bowing their heads and murmuring over their beads, knelt on the damp ground, while a thin rain fell and someone read a message from Victor Hugo beside the freshly dug grave:

"We weep for a dead woman, but we salute an immortal one. Have we really lost her? No. The human shell conceals an idea within. George Sand was an idea. She is dead and yet she still lives."

The idea George Sand . . . To some it was the brave old troubadour with whom Flaubert had argued about literature and life. To others it was the Muse of the Republic who had called Frenchmen to the barricades in 1848. To still others it was the young wife and mother in top hat and redingote who had stood up defiantly to a hostile world.

Hugo's message, blending with the call of a nightingale in the rain-drenched trees, floated over Nohant. *"Patuit dea.* . . . We know a true goddess from her stride."

Stretching out from her own to future times, that stride has already spanned over a hundred years.

Bibliography

Babbitt, Irving. *Rousseau and Romanticism.* New York: Noonday Press, 1955.

Barine, Arvède. *Alfred de Musset.* Paris: Hachette, 1893.

Cate, Curtis. *George Sand.* Boston: Houghton Mifflin, 1975.

Cortot, Alfred. *Aspects de Chopin.* Paris: Albin Michel, 1949.

Delacroix, Eugène. *Journal.* New York: Covici, Friede, 1937.

Dostoevsky, Fëdor. *Journal d'un écrivain.* Paris: Charpentier, 1904.

Ferrá, Bartomeu. *Chopin et George Sand à Majorque.* Palma de Mallorca, 1960.

Flaubert, Gustave. *Correspondance entre George Sand et Gustave Flaubert.* Paris: Calmann Lévy, 1904.

Hauser, Arnold. *The Social History of Art*, Volume 3: *Romanticism.* New York: Alfred A. Knopf, 1951.

Heine, Heinrich. *Lutèce.* Paris: Michel Lévy Frères, 1855.

Howe, Marie Jenney. *George Sand: The Search for Love.* Garden City: Garden City Publishing Co., 1929.

Karénine, Wladimir. *George Sand: Sa vie et ses oeuvres*, 4 volumes. Paris: Plon, 1899–1926.

Lubin, George. *Album Sand.* Paris: Gallimard, 1973.

———. *George Sand en Berry*. Paris: Hachette, 1967.

———. *Nohant*. Paris: Caisse Nationale des Monuments Historiques et des Sites, 1976.

Mallet, Francine. *George Sand*. Paris: Grasset, 1976.

Maurois, André. *Lélia: The Life of George Sand*. New York: Harper & Brothers, 1953.

———. *The Titans: A Three-Generation Biography of the Dumas*. New York: Harper & Brothers, 1957.

———. *A History of France*. London: Jonathan Cape, 1949.

Musset, Alfred de. *Correspondance de George Sand et d'Alfred de Musset*. Paris: Félix Decori, 1904.

Pailleron, Marie Louise. *George Sand et les hommes de 48*. Paris: Grasset, 1953.

Raleigh, Sir Walter. *Romance*. London: Oxford University Press, 1916.

Sand, George. *Oeuvres autobiographiques*. Compiled and annotated by Georges Lubin. 2 volumes. Paris: Gallimard, 1970.

———. *Correspondance*. Compiled and annotated by George Lubin, 11 volumes. Paris: Garnier, 1964–1976.

———. *Autour de la table*. Paris: Michel Lévy Frères, 1876.

———. *Questions d'art et de littérature*. Paris: Calmann Lévy, 1882.

Séché, Léon. *La Jeunesse dorée sous Louis-Philippe*. Paris: Mercure de France, 1910.

Simond, Charles. *La Vie parisienne à travers le XIXe siècle*. 2 volumes. Paris: Plon-Nourrit, 1900.

Sitwell, Sacheverell. *Liszt*. Boston: Houghton Mifflin, 1934.

Vincent, Louise. *George Sand et le Berry*. Paris: Edouard Champion, 1919.

Winwar, Frances. *The Life of the Heart: George Sand and Her Times.* Berne/Paris: Phoenix, 1947.

Zweig, Stefan. *Balzac.* New York: Viking, 1946.

The English titles of George Sand's works which appear in the text in italics are titles of translations available in some American libraries.

Index

"After Reading Indiana" (Alfred de Musset), 101
Agoult, Marie d', 140–42, 144–45, 147, 149, 192
Ajasson de Grandsagne, Stéphane, 43–44
Alicia, Sister, 33–35
Alippe, Mother, 29–30, 35
Aucante, Émile, 184

Balzac, Honoré de, 2, 62–63, 70, 83–85, 87, 91–92, 149–50, 185, 194
Baudelaire, Charles, 197
Béatrix (Honoré de Balzac), 149–50
Berlioz, Hector, 142
Bernhardt, Sarah, 183
"Berrichons," 62, 69, 71–72, 79
Beyle, Henri, 109. SEE ALSO Stendhal
Blanc, Louis, 166
Bocage, Pierre, 183
Bonaparte, Jérôme, 188

Bonaparte, Louis, 178–79. SEE ALSO Napoleon III
Borie, Victor, 184
Bourges, 81, 126–27, 134–37, 144
Brault, Augustine, 161–62
Browning, Elizabeth Barrett, 179
Browning, Robert, 179
Bulletins de la République, 167
Bulletin No. 16, 173
Buloz, François, 93, 100, 108, 115–17, 139, 142–43, 151, 158–59
Byron, George Gordon, Lord, 100, 155

Caroline, 8, 15, 20, 26, 78
Cavaignac, Eugène, General, 177
Chopin, Frédéric, 2, 147–53, 155–58, 160–63
Clésinger, Auguste, 162, 164, 187
Clésinger, Nini, 187
Clésinger, Solange, 163–64, 187. *See also* Dudevant, Solange
Communist Manifesto, 170

Campagnon du tour de France, Le, 158–59
Companion of the Tour of France, The. SEE Compagnon du tour de France, Le
Comtesse de Rudolstadt, La, 160
Confession d'un enfant du siècle, La (Alfred de Musset), 123
Consuelo, 160
Contes d'une grand-mère, 201
Corambé, 24, 27
Countess of Rudolstadt, The. SEE Comtesse de Rudolstadt, La
Country Waif, The. SEE François le Champi
Croisset, 195
Czartoryska, Princess, 156

Dame aux camélias, La (Alexandre Dumas the younger), 188
Dames Augustines, Convent of the, 28–39, 67
Daniella, La, 187
Delacroix, Eugène, 121, 148, 155, 162
Deschartres, 15–16, 20, 42–46, 50, 52, 62, 70
Devil's Pool, The. SEE Mare au diable, La
Didier, Charles, 141
Dorval, Marie, 69, 98
Dostoevsky, Fëdor, 198
Droll Stories (Honoré de Balzac), 85
Dudevant, Aurore. SEE Sand, George
Dudevant, Aurore (granddaughter of George Sand), 194, 201
Dudevant, Baron, 49–50
Dudevant, Casimir, 49–59, 61, 63, 65–66, 72, 74, 80–81, 89, 91, 93, 108–109, 124–26, 134–39, 193
Dudevant, Lina (Calamatta), 192–94

Dudevant, Marc-Antoine, 193
Dudevant, Maurice, 52, 54, 63, 65, 72, 79–80, 82, 109, 124, 134–35, 137, 139, 141, 144, 151–53, 155–56, 160–62, 164–65, 167, 179, 183–84, 187, 192–94
Dudevant, Solange, 59, 63, 65, 72, 79–80, 82, 89–90, 93–94, 109, 124, 135, 137, 139–40, 144, 151–53, 155–56, 160–62. SEE ALSO Clésinger, Solange
Dudevant, Titite, 201
Dumas, Alexandre, the elder, 189
Dumas, Alexandre, the younger, 2, 98, 188–90, 197, 201–202
Dupin, Aurore. SEE Sand, George
Dupin de Francueil, Mme., 6, 8, 12–13, 15–17, 19–20, 22–28, 33, 28–40, 42, 44–47
Dupin, Louis, 9–13, 15
Dupin, Hippolyte, 8, 13, 15–17, 20, 22, 41, 52–53, 58–59, 65–66, 72, 80, 194
Dupin, Maurice, 5–6, 8, 10–13, 15–17, 24, 44, 74, 137
Dupin, Sophie, 4–6, 8–13, 15–17, 19–20, 24–28, 33, 38, 40, 42, 45, 47–48, 50, 52, 78, 81, 137, 144–46, 189
Dupin de Francueil, Mme., 6, 8, 12–13, 15–17, 19–20, 22–28, 33, 28–40, 42, 44–47
Dupuy, Ernest, 164
Duris-Dufresne, François, 74–75
Duteil, Alexis, 125, 136
Duvernet, Charles, 59, 61

Eliot, George, 198
Elle et Lui, 123
Europe littéraire, L', 104

Figaro, 74, 76–77, 87, 90, 93
Flaubert, Gustave, 2, 194–95, 197, 199, 201–203

Fleurs du mal, Les (Charles Baudelaire), 197
Fleury, Alphonse, 59, 69
Flowers of Evil (Charles Baudelaire). SEE *Fleurs du mal, Les*
François le Champi, 182–83
Fuller, Margaret, 198

Gargilesse, 188
Genius of Christianity (René de Chateaubriand), 42
Goethe, Johann von, 155

Heine, Heinrich, 142
Histoire de ma vie, 183
History of My Life. SEE *Histoire de ma vie*
Homme de neige, L', 184
Horace, 159–60
Hugo, Victor, 69, 96, 98, 185, 203
Hugo, Mme. Victor, 96
Hunchback of Notre Dame (Victor Hugo), 69
Hypochrondriac, The (Molière). SEE *Malade imaginaire, Le*

Indiana, 88–95
Intimate Journal. SEE *Journal intime*
Ivanhoe (Walter Scott), 185

Jacques, 115
Journal des Goncourt, 190
Journal intime, 119

Kératry, Auguste de, 74–75

Laborde, Baron de, 39–40
La Châtre, 16, 43, 45, 53, 59, 125, 136–37, 139
Lafayette, Marquis de, 78
Lamartine, Alphonse de, 166, 171–72, 174
Lambert, Eugène, 184
Lamennais, Félicité de, Abbé, 128–29, 132, 141–43

Latouche, Hyacinthe de, 74, 76–77, 82, 87, 90–93
Ledru-Rollin, Alexandre, 166–67, 172, 174
Lélia, 95–96, 98–99, 101, 103–105, 126, 198
Leroux, Pierre, 141, 156, 159
Letters of a Traveller. SEE *Lettres d'un voyageur*
Lettres à Marcie, 143
Lettres d'un voyageur, 116, 132
Liszt, Franz, 2, 119–20, 132, 140–41, 144–45, 147–49, 192
Little Fadette. SEE *Petite Fadette, La*
Locke, John, 42
Louis-Philippe, King, 67, 76–77, 128, 134, 166
Lucrezia Floriani, 161

Madame Bovary (Auguste Flaubert), 194
Mademoiselle La Quintinie, 187
Madrid, 8–9
Maîtres mosaïstes, Les, 144
Majorca, 151–53
Malade imaginaire, Le (Molière), 37–38
Manceau, Alexandre, 184–85, 187–88, 192–94
Mare au diable, La, 161
Marquis de Villemer, Le, 190
Marx, Karl, 170–71
Master Mosaic-Workers, The. SEE *Maîtres mosaïstes, Les*
Mauprat, 124, 143–44
Melun, 48, 53
Mérimée, Prosper, 97, 99
Michel de Bourges, 126–32, 134–36, 138–40, 144
Mickiewicz, Adam, 142–43
Molière, 37–38
Monde, Le, 142–43
Monster Trial, 128–29, 132, 139, 141

Montaigne, Michel de, 54
Montlevic, Vicomtesse de, 39–40
Murat, Joachim, General, 8–10
Musset, Alfred de, 2, 99–101, 103, 105–19, 121, 123–24

Napoleon Bonaparte, 8–9, 23
Napoleon III, 180, 188, 190, 194.
    SEE ALSO Bonaparte, Louis
Nohant, 12–13, 16, 19–20, 22, 24, 40–47, 50–52, 59, 61–63, 80, 82–83, 117–18, 124–26, 134–37, 139, 144–45, 149, 155–56, 161, 167, 175, 183–85, 187–89, 192, 195, 197, 201–202

Paganini, Niccoló, 78
Pagello, Pietro, 113–15, 117
Pagello, Roberto, 114–15
Papet, Gustave, 59, 69
Pascal, Blaise, 42
Petite Fadette, La, 182
Planche, Gustave, 104
Pleyel, Camille, 151, 153
Potocka, Countess, 156
Prémord, Abbé de, 36
Presse, La, 182
Pyat, Félix, 69

Raspail, François, 129
Red and the Black, The (Stendhal), 109
Regnault, Émile, 69
Revue de Paris, 75, 93
Revue des Deux Mondes, 93, 100, 104, 108, 121, 132, 142, 159
Revue indépendante, 159
Roëttiers du Plessis, 48–49, 53–54
Rose et Blanche (with Jules Sandeau), 83, 87, 89
Rousseau, Jean-Jacques, 17, 42, 61

Sainte-Beuve, Charles Augustin, 92, 96–100, 106, 121, 124, 194

Saint-Simon, Claude Henri de, 69, 93
Sand, George: and Chopin, 147–53, 155–58, 160–63; and Mérimée, 97, 99; and Michel de Bourges, 126–32, 138–40, 144; and Musset, 99–101, 103, 105–19, 121, 123–24; and Sandeau, 59, 61, 69, 72, 75, 77–80, 82–83, 85, 87, 89–91, 95; convent life, 28–38; early years, 1–2, 4–6, 8, 13, 15–17, 19–20, 22, 24–26; flight from Spain, 11–13; friendship with Aurélien de Sèze, 56–57; influence on other writers, 198–99; influence of Sophie, 8, 10, 19, 45; literary career, 72, 74–78, 81–83, 87–96, 98–99, 103–105, 116, 119, 123–24, 139, 142–43, 151, 158–61, 164, 182–83, 187–88, 190; marriage to Casimir, 51–59, 61, 63, 65; Revolution of 1848, 164–68, 170–77, 180; rivalry between Sophie and Mme. Dupin, 17, 19, 24, 29, 38; Romantic movement, 2, 61, 66, 143, 148, 197–98; separation trial, 137–39; wearing men's clothes, 44–46, 71; women's rights, 1–3
Sandeau, Jules, 59, 61, 69, 72, 75, 77–80, 82–83, 85, 87, 89–91, 95, 149
Saxe, Maurice, Count de, 5–6, 65, 164
Schoelcher, Victor, 142
Sèze, Aurélien de, 56–57, 61, 138
Snow Man, The. SEE Homme de Neige, L'
Social Contract (Jean-Jacques Rousseau), 42
"Souvenir" (Alfred de Musset), 107, 123

Spiridion, 151
Stendhal, 109–10

Tales of a Grandmother. SEE *Contes d'une grand-mère*
Teresa, Sister, 33
Three Musketeers, The (Alexandre Dumas the elder), 189
Tocqueville, Alexis de, 174–75, 177

Uncle Tom's Cabin (Harriet Beecher Stowe), 180

Valentine, 93–94
Valldemosa, 153
Véron, Louis, 75
Viardot, Louis, 159
Viardot, Pauline, 160
Vigny, Alfred de, 98
Villeneuve, René de, 46–47
Voltaire, 17
Vraie République, La, 175

Whitman, Walt, 199

211